Why Should I Learn to Speak *Italian*?
The strugglers' guide to "*la bella lingua*"

Gerry Dubbin

Copyright 2016 © Gerry Dubbin
All rights reserved

No part of this book may be copied, reproduced, adapted, stored in a retrieval system, communicated or transmitted in any form or by any means without prior written permission from the author. All inquiries should be made to the author via the web address below.

Contact the author:
gerrydub@gmail.com
http://hourigan.co/authors/gerry-dubbin

Proofreading and production by Hourigan & Co.
http://hourigan.co

ISBNs
978-0-9945986-0-8 (pbk)
978-0-9945986-1-5 (e-book)

Set in Linux Libertine

Dedication:
This book is dedicated to those students of Italian still striving to achieve some fluency in *la bella lingua*. Whatever level of fluency you eventually manage to attain, always remember to enjoy the journey, it is well worth the effort.

Dedizione:
Questo libro è dedicato a gli studenti di Italiano ancora cercando per realizzare alcuni scioltezza nella bella lingua. Qualunque sia il livello di scorrevolezza quando eventualmente si riescono, a raggiungere sempre ricordare di godersi il viaggio, la sua vale la pena.

Riconoscimento:
a Pierina Dalle Nogare, una bella signora, l'ispirazione per i miei sforzi per diventare un altoparlante migliore della lingua italiano.

About the author

Gerry Dubbin spent the first eighteen years of his life in Harehills, a working-class suburb of Leeds, principal city of Yorkshire in the north of England. As a boy, he aspired to becoming a writer, a profession that circumstances put out of his reach. Instead, he entered the apparel manufacturing industry as a learner tailor. He studied apparel and textile design at the Leeds College of Technology, emerging with the highest national qualifications, including the prestigious English Silver Medal.

Following two years of compulsory national service in the RAF, and seeing few future prospects in austerity-bound post-war Britain, he decided to migrate to Australia in 1959.

Following a number of years working as apparel designer in Melbourne, during which he was responsible for establishing Australia's first apparel-industry school of technology at the Melbourne College of Textiles, he joined the Australian Wool Board—later the Australian Wool Corporation—and was eventually appointed as the corporation's international marketing director, based in New York. Since returning to Australia in the late 1970s, he has held senior management positions in the apparel, textiles and timber industries. He later went on to establish a successful signage and architectural lighting company.

Following a bitter but successfully fought dispute with a

prominent Melbourne real-estate company at the Victorian Civil & Administrative Tribunal, he was appointed as an independent consumer advocate in the real-estate field, a role that resulted in his first book, *Smoke & Mirrors, Egos & Illusions: The World of Real Estate*.

Ultimately, he decided that it was time to step away from the executive jungle, and rekindle his boyhood desire to become a published writer. *Why Should I Learn to Speak Italian?* is his fourth book.

He currently resides in Hastings, a small town located on the Mornington Peninsula's eastern shore, 60 km south east of Melbourne.

Also by Gerry Dubbin

Smoke & Mirrors, Egos & Illusions: The World of Real Estate
Conversations with a Small Boy
Liner Cruising: Your Guide to Travels Afloat

WHY SHOULD I LEARN TO SPEAK *ITALIAN*?

Contents

Prelude 1
    To start at the beginning 5
    A practical guide 12
1. The student returns – June 2015 19
    Italian language services 22
    A popular subject 27
2. Hopes, realities and questions 31
    A guide to learning Italian 34
    It's like hitting up against a wall 38
    Why study Italian in the first place? 40
    Another good reason to study Italian 43
3. Thinking in Italian 47
    I have a cold 52
    More about learning to think in Italian 55
    Did you try studying French in school? 59
    Language – The expression of a country's soul 61

4. Alice in Wonderland. 63
    Excited anticipation 64
    Italian media. 67
    The Italian way 70
    That certain something… 72
    The *passegiata*. 74
    Preferences. 76
    Feeling the need 78
5. Origins and birth of 'Standard' Italian 83
    Origins. 84
    How modern Italian developed. 86
    National and linguistic unification 88
    Standard Italian, anyone? 89
6. Where to from here? 93
    Starting out. 95
    Italian grammar is so different 96
7. After language school … what then? 103
    Universita per Stranieri, Perugia Italy 105
    More language school. 112
    Other learning options 113
8. Isn't there a quicker way?. 117
    The news here. 120

    If you cannot spend time in Italy 122

    Organising your self-study programme 125

    The use of textbooks. 126

    Audio, radio and newspapers 126

    And if one is a little older?. 132

9. Some answers and activities 135

    Try to spend some time in Italy 135

    Ask a lot of questions 137

    Try 'letting go of the bar' 139

10. Putting things together 141

    U3A's Italian language programme 143

    Buy a good book on Italian grammar. 146

    Don't be afraid to talk to yourself. 147

    Why not consider a language course in Italy?. 152

    Speaking Italian – In Italy 154

    TIM and my iPhone 157

11. Three months in Treviso – 2015 161

    Why choose Treviso?. 163

    Quasi Trevigiano. 165

    Organising the project 166

    Renting accommodation in Italy. 167

12. Seeing and doing around Treviso 171
    Treviso – A brief history. 171
    Piazza dei Signori. 175
    A unique fountain, medieval alleyways 176
    Pescheria, antique water mills. 177
    After all that … did my Italian improve? 178
    In conclusion 181
13. References and information 185
    Articles: Benefits of learning a second language 187
    Italian courses. 194
    Pimsleur Italian. 198
    Italian textbooks 199
    Some books on Italian grammar 199
    Two useful books written in English 202
    Italian learning systems online. 204
    Italian learning system reviews 205
    Sites detailing Italian schools and services in Italy . . . 206
    The Veneto and the province of Treviso 207

Prelude

"Why should I learn to speak Italian?" An interesting question this and one that has occupied my mind many times, especially when I found myself struggling to understand yet another section of difficult-to-learn vocabulary in my well-thumbed Italian grammar textbook.

In addition to the 60 million odd authentic native Italians currently living in and around that picturesque and historic peninsula, there remains a large number of *stranieri* (foreigners) also intent on gaining access to their language. A few of us are known to have studied from time to time in Italy, while most have of necessity to do their studying at a variety of foreign-based language schools.

If you, like me, are an aficionado of that melodic, romantic language – you are not alone. At this very moment there are sure to be many more just like us somewhere across the world, all treading a hopeful path toward being able to both speak and read it with understanding. Some perhaps may even aspire to gaining full fluency in Italian – a considerable achievement, bearing in mind some of the difficulties to be found when trying to decode the language in written form.

The question as to why there are so many non-Italians seeking to become Italian speakers is also worth pursuing, with a variety of opinions on offer – some pointing to differing reasons. One of the foremost must be that many non-Italians continue to find Italy a highly desirable place to visit – but does that make the Italian language so worthy of the struggle to possess it?

That is but the beginning. Just Google the question that forms the title to this book and you will open up a whole world of information. You will see many reasons given as to why learning the language can be such fun, plus many more from a growing number of proprietary websites, all seeking to push themselves and their educational products to the fore. Many of these feel the need to offer all kinds of promises to potential purchasers of their Italian courses, some along the lines of "Why Italian is easy, (you could become) fluent in 3 months" or variations on the theme of "learn Italian in 30 days." Other sites offer up a range of answers to questions surrounding the learning of Italian, "10 top reasons to learn Italian" or "Top 10 myths about learning Italian." So it goes on, web page following web page.

I well remember when I first decided to commit myself to learning Italian. At the time, it presented as a relatively easy language to learn and eventually perhaps one even possible to master. Easy, that is, if I had allowed myself to believe all that was written about learning to speak the language, particularly much of the stuff contained in most of the advertising blurbs being put out by various Italian schools and a whole host of other offerings of teaching expertise and other kinds of assistance that are made on the Internet.

The reality though turned out to be somewhat different. Three months following my first foray into the world of Italian, it was beginning to prove more complex than I had at first envisaged – at least it seemed so to this long-time speaker of English. And the time scale required? That also turned out to be much longer than the 'few months' promised so glibly by the school at which I first commenced my studies.

Like so many before and after me, I ventured forth, expectantly clutching a brace of brand-new textbooks on Italian verbs, grammar, and anything else I thought might be of use to me during my quest. I had in fact, without realising it, ventured upon a voyage of discovery that I am sure will continue to spur me on for the rest of my learning days.

Having bought or borrowed a copy of this book, perhaps you too have an interest in things Italian. Or perhaps you are currently working your own way through an Italian language course you are attending in a country outside Italy. In that case, you too will have also started out on your search for some Italian language skills.

If you are a student of Italian, then perhaps you have reached a stage in your studies where you now find yourself beginning to doubt if you will ever be able to progress as far as you had originally hoped. I know I at times found myself in such a situation, where it began to feel as though I was about to hit an unyielding barrier, a virtual wall that was barring my progress.

Even following just a few months of tuition, it was starting to seem as though I had arrived at a stage in my Italian studies where, despite all my efforts to learn, absorb and hold onto a useful range of verbs, grammar and other obviously important stuff that I had been learning to date, I was finding it more and more difficult to recall and use much of what I had learned just a few weeks before. I was struggling to bring to mind enough of what I had learned, in the hope of putting together even the simplest form of conversation in Italian.

While I was able to pick up some Italian words and phrases, I was unable to absorb and understand much of a conversation being offered by an Italian speaker. I felt that I was being held back by what seemed like an unyielding and immovable force, around which I could not pass. I lacked the capacity to absorb and understand what was being said by the other party, sufficiently quickly to put together enough learned vocabulary to enable the offering of an intelligent reply.

I later learned that these feelings of hitting up against a wall are common during the learning of any second language, particularly for an adult student. Eventually I also learned that most, if not all students would find themselves in something of a struggle, this particularly when trying to make the transition from what to date had been an adult lifetime of speaking English, to being able to carry on even a simple, coherent conversation in Italian.

The process involved with the learning of Italian, particularly if an adult English speaker, can prove to be a long, sometimes frustrating one. Believe me, I know, hence the title of this book, which is not just a question about the usefulness of learning Italian, but also an expression of my earlier bewilderment. "Why on earth am I trying to learn Italian?" I sometimes used to ask myself.

For this long-time speaker of English the task at times certainly proved something of a challenge. Often I was left more than a little frustrated when finding myself trying to remember some of the more difficult word combinations I needed to include when constructing a sentence that just might (and I stress the word *might* here) make some sense to a passing Italian – at least one having the patience to stop and listen to what I had to say.

The subtitle of this book highlights the fact that the task of learning Italian can prove to be something of a struggle. I will readily admit that the word *struggle* is appropriate to use here. At times I even found myself in danger of sinking into a self-made mire of frustration, emitting a negative and unhelpful groan from time to time, as I ventured forth on my quest to becoming a reasonably proficient speaker of *la bella lingua* (the beautiful language).

To start at the beginning

Let's start with the question "Why should anyone travelling to Italy, either on a vacation or for business, need to know much more than just a smattering of Italian words and maybe the addition of a couple of short phrases?"

This is a question of some relevance, particularly for anyone treading the much-travelled route to one or other of the many tourist-attracting locations scattered around one of the world's most fascinating countries. Many of the locals in Italy do possess what could be regarded as a working level of English, sufficient generally to enable them to speak it well enough to meet the needs of their employment in one or other of a multitude of restaurants, pizza shops, bars, boutiques and other commercial operations seeking to provide services to foreign tourists.

With many thousands of visitors from around the world trying to gain a working knowledge of Italian, and others having the desire to speak more than just a few words of the language, the consensus seems to be that relatively few English speakers will get very far beyond the basics of Italian. This means that the majority of those starting out on their journey will more than likely find it difficult to attain much beyond a basic or possibly an 'intermediate' level of understanding. While others may go on to reach a higher level as a result of their studies, enabling them to become capable of maintaining a conversation in passable Italian, few are expected to eventually arrive at what might have been their original dream of full fluency.

Another question you might like to ponder: "Do you recall why or how the bug prompting you to want to learn how to speak Italian first got into your system?"

For me the desire to be able to communicate in Italian started out in the form of what I think best described as a 'magnificent obsession'. A case of which I still find difficult to ignore following many years visiting Italy.

That obsession had its start when, as a much younger man, I was working at the centre of the Australian textile and fashion industry with the Australian Wool Board.[1] One fateful day during the mid 1970s found me having just arrived at Milan's Linate airport, at the start of my very first visit to Italy.

At the time, apart from one or two words and a few of the usual short and not very well expressed Italian phrases, my grasp of the local language was to say the least, practically non-existent.

To me in those days, spoken Italian presented as a mysterious jumble of melodious words, a mysterious language that had hung around since ancient Roman times. When spoken by an Italian, the language appeared to flow and bubble along with the speed of a mountain stream in the early springtime. Funny thing that, one or two of my Italian friends these days have also said something similar about spoken English, particularly when

---

[1] The Australian Wool Board was a semi-government authority responsible for the promotion of Australian wool and wool products.

they find themselves trying to understand at least something of what a native speaker of English is saying – a speaker who in all probability happens to be rattling along at full speed, words blurring into one another.

According to some of my Italian friends, English is a difficult language to understand, this more so should the speaker have a strong local accent. It just goes to show perhaps that when it comes to anyone trying to learn a second language, perceptions can be decidedly one-sided!

The Italian language, particularly during my first few visits to the country, was spoken with such rapidity that individual words were difficult to pick up. It also seemed that any hope of me eventually becoming capable of discerning the meaning of a short phrase here and there was remote. While occasionally I was able to pick out a word or two, the rest of what was being said became lost. Even having undertaken some tuition before making my first visit to Italy, by the time I had found myself able to pick out a word here and there, the conversation had passed on leaving me wallowing frustratingly in its wake, along with a growing feeling of inadequacy.

I was newly arrived in a foreign country. There I was, a complete stranger, excitedly looking forward to my very first taste of a country and people that not many years earlier, as a boy growing up and living through the dangerous days of the Second World War, I had regarded as being alien and avowed enemies. Italians in those days were on the other side of a global war that threatened my very existence.

It's interesting to note here, just how the passage of time often serves to change many of our earlier personal perceptions and prejudices.

On this my first visit to Italy I was, as you may have already gathered, English born and an earlier immigrant who, back in 1959 and among many thousands of others, had arrived in Australia as a £10 'Pommie migrant'. I eventually settled in Melbourne, someone to whom Italy and Italians at the time were represented in the form of the family who owned the Universita café in Lygon Street. They and many others like them – most also relatively recent Italian immigrants, having settled in and around the northern Melbourne suburbs. Lygon Street, located in the inner suburb of Carlton, was a region of the city that had become known far and wide as 'little Italy'.

Having just arrived in Italy on my first business trip, I had been picked up at the airport by an employee from the Milan office of my employer's associate company in Italy, the International Wool Secretariat. This was closely followed, over ensuing days, by meetings with English-speaking executives representing some of Italy's leading fashion designers, textile and apparel manufacturers. My visit to Italy was part of a programme of visits to other leading European mills and fashion houses. Not being a speaker of Italian I had, of necessity, to be accompanied at every meeting by an English-speaking Italian employee from the Milan office.

At the time, there appeared little real need for me to possess much more than a partial understanding of the local language. Why indeed should I have had any interest in learning more, other than perhaps the gaining of a couple of words of greeting, goodbye and thanks? – limited language skills that could perhaps prove useful during a short, busy business trip, later to be followed by the usual wander around various tourist spots and visits to shops and expensive boutiques in Rome and Milan.

It was only later one evening during that first visit, on going out to dinner and meeting up with a crowd of friends of my new

Italian business colleagues, a meal followed by a visit to a local discotheque, that I found myself partnering an attractive Italian girl.

Although unable to invite her to dance in so many words, I found myself, more through desperation than anything else, having to resort to gesturing as a means of inviting her to join me on the dance floor. Luckily, she seemed to understand my dilemma and, probably as she had nothing better to do, she accepted my invitation.

My Milan-based colleagues assisted in my introduction a little here, explaining, as if such an explanation was actually needed, that I was a non-Italian-speaking visitor from Australia. Luckily for me, even with her lack of English and mine of Italian, we managed to find ourselves as dancing partners for the rest of the evening. Via gestures more than anything else, we also found ourselves able to engage in a level of communication which I think best described as being more in the way of instinctive as opposed to being fully understood on either side. There was so much I would like to have been able to discuss with both her and her Italian friends, but having virtually no vocabulary with which to do so, it became a frustrating case of an evening lost, at least when it came to verbal communication.

My last weekend in and around Milan was spent as an invited guest at the home of one of my new-found colleagues, a quaint house complete with fruit trees, a large vegetable and grapevine filled back garden, plus chickens and a pet goat. The house was located in a small, leafy township just outside Milan.

My weekend there, while enjoyable as a new experience, which it certainly was, proved to be a struggle when it came to conversation. The only person in the family other than my English-speaking colleague was his mother. She could speak some English, hers being learned, or more probably picked up, during some years past in her role as a teacher at a local *scuola secondaria* (secondary school).

With some helpful assistance from *mamma*, I eventually got to learn a little simple Italian. During the process, my new-found colleague and his wife were able to improve their English a little, just sufficient on both our parts to keep us going in what turned out to be a continuing friendship that lasted until I left what later became the Australian Wool Corporation.

From Milan, I later travelled south. As I was on my own for most of the time, my lack of usable Italian turned what should have been a really enjoyable experience into something less: a tour in which my inability to communicate served to reduce what should have been an interesting and unrestrained visit to a mainly silent and often frustrating one.

On returning to Melbourne following my first visit to Italy, and with the possibility of looking forward to an ongoing friendship with new Italian business associates, I resolved not only to get myself to the point where I could at least say a few useful things in Italian, but also with the intention of eventually becoming a reasonably proficient communicator, reaching at least the upper limitations of someone unable to live in Italy on a permanent basis.

This, therefore, was the beginning of what for me became an important, absorbing and at times frustrating journey. It is also a story that sometimes ambled its erratic way, particularly in the early stages, during which I failed to make much progress – particularly when it came to Italian conversation. I was motivated, but so many other aspects of my personal and business life kept getting in the way. Progress with my language studies became aimless, fragmented and often confused, resulting in me gaining little that was long lasting.

A few years passed, during which I only just managed to get by on subsequent visits to Europe. This was assisted by the addition of an Italian phrase here and there, also with some new verbs that I had been able to pick up and retain along the way. This usually occurred in a haphazard way, without having the opportunity to spend more than a week or so at any one time visiting Italy during any of my subsequent visits.

I occasionally managed to continue my Italian studies, but because other distractions constantly intervened, and later when I began to find that the kind of tuition I had accessed to date was becoming stalled, I eventually found myself seeking some other, more practical means of study. This eventually became a search that led to the development of a programme of 'self-tuition', one in which I sought to incorporate supporting practical exercises and learning aids, which I then started to use – when the opportunity and spare time presented itself.

It had become obvious, by that time, that if I was going to advance much further without having the advantage of spending time actually living in Italy, I needed to find a more flexible, systematic approach to language acquisition, that could be accommodated alongside an active business career.

As the programme slowly developed, it eventually proved possible to gain an acceptable level of language proficiency, even working outside the established school-based system. By 'established system' I am referring here to the system of language tuition generally regarded as being the only practical means available in Australia at the time capable of providing access to the language, other than actually deciding to live in Italy.

This eventually culminated in 2014 with the decision to evaluate the level of language proficiency I had been able to gain as a result of my self-tuition style of language learning. Having spent a whole year using the system that evolved, it seemed that the best way of proving if my efforts had borne fruit would be to actually take up temporary residence in Italy. To do so seemed the only way to determine whether I had been successful in my quest to extend my ability to communicate in Italian.

A practical guide

What follows, apart from chronicling my earlier unsteady progress toward achieving a reasonable degree of conversational proficiency in Italian, are guidelines that should be of some interest to others aiming to become better speakers of the language – some perhaps experiencing similar difficulties to those I found myself coming up against.

It is useful to record here that the search for learning aids and other components of the self-tuition programme that eventuated, often became complex. This was due mainly to there being so many possibilities and choices needing to be made from among what at times proved an almost impossibly broad range of language learning services, many featuring on the Internet. It soon became clear that while there were many different kinds and levels of services and learning aids from which to choose, it would be necessary from a practical standpoint to limit the range and number of study elements to a few, using only those proving to offer the best in terms of their range, ease of use and area of specialty.

Following a great deal of what could best be termed a 'taste-and-try' style of research into then available Italian learning aids, it eventually became possible to pinpoint, trial and finally isolate an effective system of support activities, a personal study programme that proved capable of meeting my learning needs.

The issue of self-imposed discipline, alongside the use of selected learning aids was of importance here. As I and possibly other adult students of Italian studying outside Italy will have already found from a financial and time standpoint, it is rarely a practical proposition to commit oneself to attendance solely at an established language school – certainly not on a full-time basis.

I had also found that there are limitations to the capacity of the usual kind of language school available in Australia to provide a great deal beyond what is generally known as intermediate level in Italian tuition. This became particularly apparent because my desire was to be able to advance to a higher level of proficiency with conversational Italian. The cost alone to rely solely on school-based study would be prohibitive, with few, other than a young student intent on the academic study of Italian, gaining much benefit from a predominantly classroom-based option, particularly when it comes to gaining the ability to speak well.

Seeking to move beyond intermediate level at an established school, usually supported by school-specified study books and written homework, has its limitations. When trying to move beyond that point, adult English-speaking students similar to me will more than likely find that to do so a higher, sometimes elusive, often subtle and 'self-engaging' level of learning is required. It will gradually become clear that the skills needed from here on in are better sought after outside the limitations of an often-crowded classroom and one or maybe two formal tuition sessions per week.

It took some time before I was able to isolate the learning aids that proved most useful. By that, I mean the kind of aids best able to assist retention of and confidence with the range of vocabulary needed to hold my own with a normal paced everyday kind of conversation.

The usual language school classroom at best is a relatively static kind of learning environment that relies mainly on the use of texts and similar forms of information transfer. When it comes to gaining the higher level of skills required to enable a student of Italian to begin to speak freely, it is a system lacking much. This is particularly so when the need is more toward one of stimulating a student's ability to think more in Italian, while acquiring a much wider range of vocabulary – at the same time gaining the confidence to use it.

Gaining the skills necessary to enable a student to actually become able to speak Italian well suggests that once having gained the necessary grammar, verbs and a range of vocabulary, a different kind of learning process is required from here on. It is a more creative process, capable of encouraging the retention of a more advanced set of language skills, which are very different in scope and purpose to what has been learned and absorbed to date.

It may well be that statements such as those offered above will sound a little strange to some language teachers, 'experts' who may still take the view that it is possible to gain the necessary levels of conversational Italian by continuing to attend a classroom style format.

Experience has taught me differently. I found instead that a teaching environment that meant me having to share one tutor, once or twice per week, with a group of other students all vying for the tutor's attention, was not the best environment within which to be gaining the ability to absorb the range of skills needed to speak Italian with confidence.

As noted earlier, there are a whole host of Italian language services and aids to learning to be found via the Internet. Each year sees more being added, either in the form of new learning programmes or other associated learning aids. Some appear in the form of new kinds of smartphone, laptop and desktop computer based applications, while others concentrate on teaching the language via an oral format. Some applications offer innovative language translation services.

It is interesting to note here how so many established language schools still go about advertising their courses, many claiming to be capable of "teaching you to speak Italian in just a few, easy lessons". Such an attractive way of promoting their services I found to be more than a little disingenuous as I began to find that the learning and retention of Italian were going to take much longer than "a few easy lessons". I should also add here that some Internet offers also include promises similar to their school-based colleagues.

As a lifelong speaker of English I found like many others before me, that trying to learn to speak Italian but living thousands of kilometres away from the country, is not as easy as many providers of language learning systems like to make out. I tried to learn the way most schools try to teach the language, but found that while up to a point they were successful, to go on from there did not work sufficiently well enough for me.

At this point I think it also important to state that what follows is offered, not from someone trying to sell a 'fast to learn' Italian course or an affordable and 'fun-filled' series of learning aids. The following pages instead describe how, following a period of neglectful study, I managed to come up with an alternative way by which to advance toward gaining a useful level of Italian language proficiency.

At times this narrative may be more accurately described as an acknowledgement of sorts, particularly so when discussing some of the more difficult or negative aspects of language learning, as experienced by a reasonably intelligent adult native English-speaking student, who at times found himself struggling with Italian.

The latter is important, as I have come to understand, as a result of my own efforts aimed at learning a second language, that there is much to be gained and learned from the experiences of others. What follows therefore is offered as the personal experiences of a student – one who continues to study.

I was something of a struggling student to start with, but later began to feel a sense of growing satisfaction when at last I found myself able to communicate with a reasonable level of success. I intend to continue studying Italian and trying to extend my capacity to speak the language, using the methods and learning aids later to be discussed.

Should you be a student of Italian, the following pages should provide some useful pointers, suggestions and examples by which you can extend your knowledge a little more about Italy and Italians. Much more also on the subject of learning to speak Italian, including a way of study and a range of practices designed to assist the gaining of Italian language skills – even if living half the world away from Italy.

Also included later are details of one of the more varied and interesting parts of that fascinating country, a province known as 'the Veneto'. I will also include a short discussion on something often referred to in a general way as 'the Italian way of life and living', life in Italy as I have been able to experience it following many years of travel there.

It is relevant also to record here that during my early years growing up in England I knew little, and thought even less, about Italy and Italians. As a young boy and later as a pre-teenager I had little interest in or knowledge of the country, other than the fact that Britain during my boyhood was at war with Italy and Germany. During the long years of that war, I can claim to have had a passing acquaintance with the only individual considered by the locals to have a close Italian connection, not interned but living in my neighbourhood.

Angelo Granelli was the only individual claiming to be of Italian heritage that I knew of in those days, and even then only vaguely. He was the ancient and kindly local maker and supplier of tasty *gelato* (Italian-style ice cream), a delicious product well loved by we street kids, which he hawked around the local suburb of Harehills, in the Yorkshire city of Leeds.

Mr Granelli made his particular brand of gelato in one of the backrooms of his house, located not very far from my street. He sold it to we local kids and families from his green, white and red painted two-wheeled handcart and icebox that he pushed around the nearby streets, as he serenaded the local housewives with operatic airs and Italian love songs.

My impressions of things Italian were to change dramatically following my migration to Australia in 1959, where I then got to meet many immigrant Italians. Some were the owners of local coffee shops, *trattorie* (restaurants) and others, mainly work colleagues.

Over later years as a businessman, I was eventually lucky enough to be able to visit and experience some of the better-known parts of Italy on a fairly regular basis, even some regions off the well-beaten tourist track.

Over the years, I have also met up with many more of its people, listening to and trying always to absorb a little more of their melodious language. In the process, I have also managed to gain a much deeper appreciation of and for the Italian way of being.

Perhaps more importantly from a personal standpoint, I am one Australian who, from a very low base, eventually managed to become a reasonable speaker of Italian.

I am not yet fluent by any stretch of the imagination, but sufficiently capable of communicating and doing nearly everything one usually finds necessary to become involved with while visiting the country. That is a level of Italian far in advance of where I commenced my journey.

1. The student returns – June 2015

Trenitalia's *Frecciargento* (Silver Arrow) express train was at last speeding me north and further away from the daily chaos, pickpockets, beggars, crowds and tumult that seems always to swirl in and around Rome's Termini railway station. That major rail terminus always feels like it is in a constant state of being repaired, redesigned or renovated. At any time it seems also to be locked in a constant struggle, trying to keep up with the demands of an ever-increasing number of Italy's and the world's travelling public.

It was good at last to be on the train, also to find my booked seat vacant and the overhead luggage rack not packed tight with some other passenger's luggage. By the time I got myself settled down, we were well on our way north and away from the daily choking crowds thronging the platforms, cafés and waiting areas of that bustling transport hub.

Termini is an international railway station with little to be proud of when it comes to amenities, certainly those in the form of comfortable seating for the crowds of travellers usually to be found waiting for their rail connections to all points across Italy and Europe. This finds most having to sit around, usually on the floor of the main concourse or crowded into nearby cafés, as they await the arrival of rail connections or passengers.

I was by now well settled into my seat and starting to think in a more detailed way about my plan to spend the next three months living Italian-style in an ancient Italian city. As the train thundered smoothly north I also began brooding over the question of whether or not I would be successful when it came to my reasons for making this trip to Italy.

Would the final touches of my plan to improve my Italian language skills prove to be yet another couple of months of wasted time, not forgetting the waste of hard to acquire funds? Time and money indulgently expended in the perhaps false hope of improving my capacity to understand and converse in Italian with a greatly improved level of fluency.

I was looking forward with some hope, following not very far off a decade of relatively disordered and frequently neglected study. I was now hoping that following the past year or so of regular, concentrated study, I should now be in a position to make good progress toward my goal of eventually becoming a competent Italian speaker.

I was also at the time thinking about how my plan to rent an apartment in the northern Italian city of Treviso would work out, particularly once there having also committed myself to commencing my stay with a three-week study course at a local language school.

The aim here was to cap off the past year of self-study and practice, a year during which I had used a variety of aids and other practical exercises, carefully researched and selected specifically for their capacity to provide me with a more effective route by which to gain and retain a broader range of Italian vocabulary. Following implementation of the programme of study that resulted, this visit and my planned three-month-long stay in Italy were intended to prove if my self-study regime had been successful.

I had decided to commence my visit with a three-week

period of formal studies, these intended mainly as a means of brushing up my Italian grammar, a continuing weak link for me in the past, in addition to gaining some time in which to reorient myself to the pace of living in Italy. I was also looking forward to having more practice with Italian conversation, practice that would assist me when it came to communicating with local residents, and of course any Italian-speaking foreign visitors I happened to meet up with during my stay.

This visit was intended to be much different to the others I had made to this historic, intriguing country and its people, over past years.

I was no longer a widely travelled businessman; nor was I visiting Italy this time as a tourist. This was a visit with a definite purpose in mind – one that I hoped would justify past months of research and study undertaken before making the decision to commit to three months of residency.

Would I as a result, be able to advance solidly toward my goal, or would my stay result in something less?

Three months living in any country was admittedly a relatively short period during which to expect to get close to perfecting anyone's grasp of a second language. But then, when added to years of irregular and sparse periods of study that I had involved myself in from time to time back in Australia, this time I was intent on pushing myself past the barriers I had often found myself coming up against.

This trip also presented an opportunity to test my capacity to be able to either climb over or go around some of the issues that had been blocking my progress.

My visit to Italy in 2015 had two objectives:

1. To check if my self-study programme had been effective in improving my Italian conversation skills to the point of being capable of holding a reasonably intelligent conversation with a native speaking Italian.

2. To continue working on my next book during any spare time that came my way.

Italian language services

"How had I had approached the selection of learning services and support aids used as part of my self-tuition programme?"

This had been an important element of the programme that eventuated, so perhaps I should start there...

It is reasonable to observe that educational bookshops and language schools the world overabound with all manner of textbooks dealing with Italian verbs, grammar, a whole host of language learning systems and other aids. More so on the Internet where just an hour or so of surfing will no doubt uncover many different offerings on and around the subject of how to go about learning Italian.

These usually range from tutoring services presented via Skype, advertising for various colleges, schools and a variety of other established learning institutions. Offerings also include a variety of downloadable language learning systems, usually in disc form, and translation services, many of these services being adaptable for use on an iPhone, iPad and other cellular devices. Many of these are relatively recent technical innovations, now allowing an ever-increasing flow of worldwide access to information on language services, up-to-the-minute news in a variety of languages, plus other associated educational services and aids.

The Internet, now a universally used instantaneous channel of communication has also become the means through which the promoters of a confusing array of language learning systems and associated aids are seeking to market their wares. Unfortunately the Internet offers little or no opportunity to 'taste and try' before one buys, before making a commitment to purchase.

The question here:

How useful or otherwise are some of these systems or aids to the learning of Italian? What should someone new to the study of Italian be on the lookout for and, having once decided upon one system as opposed to other competing systems, how to extract the best use from the material selected?

Not having much previous experience with a broad range of the learning systems being promoted by schools, colleges and others via the Internet, it became necessary to trial some of these, before making a choice. Questions as to the relative value of some of these systems proved illuminating. This was particularly so when it came to the need to sort out which, among the various systems and aids on offer were best suited to my needs.

How best to approach the learning of my chosen second language to the point where I could become capable of holding a reasonably intelligent conversation with a native Italian speaker? That too was another subject needing much thought.

Research, in some cases trialling and evaluation of the various language learning products and services on offer, began to result in a number of interesting and instructive discoveries.

Among the more useful services purchased and trialled, I also found that I had invested in others that eventually proved to be a waste of my time and money. Some of the offerings that I trialled in the latter category tended to base their promises of rapid access to Italian as if it was simple enough to be absorbed relatively quickly – and spoken almost instantly.

I guess the best way of describing the kind of learning offers, systems and services that I found to be less than helpful, is on the basis that a large proportion of them offered an approach to learning Italian in the same way a number of other commercial marketing organisations go about selling their own sometimes magical-sounding recipes for success. The content and depth of others was found to be shallow, and some were difficult to follow or work with.

Some of the language learning systems being marketed seemed to follow the same route as the manufacturers and marketers of analgesics regularly use to promote their products. These are products, you may recall, that consumers are being constantly exhorted to shovel down their throats, usually in the form of a tablet or potion claiming to be able to assist a sufferer of all manner of pains, to gain instant relief from a headache, back pain or some other form of physical discomfort. Other offers came in a different form promising instant success. Some promises had a disturbing similarity to the sales pitch of the sellers of pre-cooked frozen food – dishes that only require the addition of some water to a packet of stuff, or heat to a frozen pack of fish fingers or similar, requiring but a few minutes in a microwave to achieve an instant meal. Some of these are even known to describe their offerings as being of 'gourmet' standard!

Also take for example the promise to enable someone to lose a load of excess weight in a very short time, simply by paying a fee that then allows them to attend the advertiser's ultra-efficient weight-loss clinic, and/or purchase from their range of 'gourmet chef'–created, cooked and frozen foods, "all delivered direct to your home!"

These and many similar promises of almost instant success are, we are told, capable of being gained with very little in the way of physical or mental outlay on the part of the purchaser. The general theme with many such offers these days being on the basis that little effort is required on the part of the consumer.

While admittedly the sellers of analgesics, frozen foods and quick-fire weight reducing systems are not exactly comparable to the providers of Italian learning systems, some Italian schools and Internet-based sellers of Italian learning services still continue to offer their products alongside a promise that any student enrolling with them and using their particular learning system, will be able to "speak in Italian" in just a few days or weeks. One or two even go further with the claim that their students should expect to be capable of "speaking Italian after the first day!"

The kind of services being offered by any one of these language schools may well prove to be lots of fun as some claim. They may also be capable of providing access to the mysteries of Italian grammar, verbs and all the other elements of the language that a student needs to access as they progress through the initial stages of language learning.

My own and many others' experiences however, have served to demonstrate that a point in time eventually arrives, usually after a student has managed to progress to the point where they now possess what they feel to be a reasonably broad range of Italian vocabulary. Should they now wish to advance much beyond that level, may well be the point at which most will find themselves in need of a very different range of language skills training to eventually be able to speak effectively in Italian.

This is the point at which I also found that in spite of my regular attendances at classroom-based language tuition, my capacity to use what I had learned to date was falling well short of the skills required.

Anyone living outside Italy who expects to become capable of carrying on an intelligent conversation in Italian following months of classroom-based tuition is being unrealistic. For me, arriving at that stage in my Italian studies forced on me the reality that if I was to advance further toward being a reasonably proficient speaker, it would be necessary to find some other, more appropriate route along which to progress.

As a businessman at the time, travelling on a regular basis both within Australia and overseas, I could no longer afford to rely on my attendance on a weekly basis at a local language school, which incidentally was located a long way from my home. Even though the school in question was a well-recognised provider of Italian tuition, I had to accept the unpalatable fact that the kind of tuition I was then receiving was limited in its capacity to provide the necessary means toward achieving the level of language skills I was seeking. The question then became:

"What other means outside the classroom format would be capable of providing the additional level of language skills required, perhaps more important – the confidence with which to use them?"

Would it be possible for a reasonably intelligent adult to

gain the necessary skills by undertaking studies outside the usual methods and teaching techniques being offered by local language schools? Could the ready availability of a rapidly increasing range of innovative learning aids, currently being advertised on the Internet and elsewhere, offer the possibility to progress further and faster? Could the judicious use of learning aids and other forms of practice, outside the traditionally accepted format of an often-crowded classroom, provide an acceptable and practical answer?

Why wouldn't it be possible to tutor oneself using a carefully selected range of available language learning aids? Could it then as a result, eventually be possible to become a speaker of Italian, by the regular use of a range of carefully selected learning aids, employed in a controlled and disciplined way?

A lot of questions I know. I will however attempt later to describe how at least one long-time and often neglectful student of Italian, who found the usual classroom format more restricting than helpful, eventually managed to devise a self-tutoring routine that proved both practical and economic.

A popular subject

Moving aside briefly from a discussion around language learning services, it will be useful here to discuss just how much the study of the Italian language has gripped many across the world.

Judging from the number of language learning services currently on offer in bookshops, across the Internet and other media, the desire to speak Italian continues to attract an increasing number of hopeful students. What is looking like an ever-increasing demand for language learning services specialising in Italian, has also resulted in the parallel growth of individual teachers and formal language-teaching organisations, all vying for their slice of the language-teaching pie.

One site on the Internet recently put the number of Italian learners worldwide at a mind-boggling 10.5 million! This figure, which even if overstated, is an indication that the learning of Italian must rank near, if not at the top of the list of preferred second languages sought after by students across the world.

The Italian language stands alongside a continuing worldwide interest in Italy as a preferred tourist destination. Italy, seemingly in preference to many other parts of Europe, continues to be visited regularly by individuals and schools seeking to study its long and multifaceted history, cuisine, art, artists and music both past and present. As a popular tourist destination the country also continues to attract many hundreds of thousands of visitors each year, possibly receiving more foreign visitors over any given period of the year than any other single tourist destination.

Small as the country is, Italy for example would come close to fitting within the borders of my relatively small home states of Victoria and Tasmania. Though it may be small in area, over many centuries Italy has exerted influence over many of the countries surrounding it, often out of all proportion to its size. This is particularly so when one considers such diverse subjects as language, religion, music, astronomy, scientific research, art, cuisine and, as a centre of advanced learning.

Italy is credited as being the country in which the first university was established. It has also served to create the desire among travellers across the world to visit, stay awhile and sometimes even managed to arouse the idea among some to actually want to live there.

Many dreamers have planned to retire to Italy, possibly with a view to writing their memoirs, while perhaps sipping on a glass or two of *vino rosso di Montepulciano*, as they gaze out across the rolling countryside from the veranda of their *villetta* (small villa) nestling among the Tuscan hills.

Italy and what the country and its culture have come to mean to many people across the world, has also prompted the desire among some, this writer included, to learn more about its history and culture, while so doing to also seek to acquire the capacity to communicate in its melodious language.

2. Hopes, realities and questions

Before proceeding further, I need to say something about some less than successful ways of going about learning to speak Italian. Something called 'Standard' Italian, that is. In particular, I want to discuss some of the problems I came up against during my studies and other issues that most other adult English-speaking students are also likely to meet up with during their Italian studies.

One important issue involved with the learning of any second language is learning how to avoid some of what I came to know as 'blockers', obstacles to progress that most students will meet up with, once embarked on their journey.

During the time I became involved with evaluating the various language courses being offered by a multitude of experts on the subject, I gradually came to realise that few were really capable of providing the total answer to any one individual student's language learning needs. This point became important as I attempted to assess the relative values of the different kinds of language learning systems and other aids then on offer – particularly as they related to the needs of adult students located a long way from Italy.

Some school-based courses or learning systems were certainly capable of providing access to a part of the picture, while others – mainly those offering the promise that a buyer of their particular system or course would find themselves capable of speaking Italian in a very short time, being less so.

The latter group appear more intent on making promises to potential clients, most of which often lead to unrealistic expectations for early success being hoped for by students taking up their offer. Claims such as these offer little in the way of reality or substance, instead promising a doubtful pathway toward eventually achieving language proficiency.

Let's face it: the only tried and true pathway toward achieving full fluency in any second language will only become a realistic goal as a result of a student deciding to immerse themselves totally in the language, culture and general everyday living. This means actually deciding to live in the country of their choice, preferably over a number of years.

One researcher and writer on the subject of language learning has suggested a level of 10,000 hours of study being the minimum required to achieve full fluency in any second language. Now that's quite a bundle of hours, when you try to work such a number out on the basis of the amount of study hours required each week, the number of months, even years that would be required for eventual success.

For more details on the suggested level of 10,000 hours of study, see articles included in the References section.

Other than the prospect of having to spend at least 10,000 or so hours in tuition and practice to become fluent – which the proposer of this level of tuition suggested applies to any foreign student – I believe that the most anyone should realistically expect to achieve, particularly if living far from Italy, is to aim at becoming what I think best termed as 'partially fluent'.

In other words, should they not have the inclination or time at their disposal to study for the 10,000 hours suggested, they would be better advised to aim for a lesser level of proficiency in their chosen language, at which they can still expect to be capable of carrying on a reasonable level of conversation. Not necessarily totally fluent, but partially so. This means getting themselves to a point in their studies that enables them to become capable of communicating with at least some confidence.

To become partially fluent in Italian can still be a rewarding experience. It all depends on how you define the terminology and how each student chooses to set their target then goes about the task – on how, eventually a student finds him or herself becoming able to apply what they have learned and absorbed when later travelling in Italy.

By using the term 'partially fluent' here, I am suggesting that it is within the capacity of any serious student to become just that, partially (usefully) fluent in Italian. Using one or two of the better thought through language courses to commence with, then moving on to a programme of disciplined self-study coupled to the use of a selection of learning aids, an acceptable level of language proficiency is possible.

If fully committed to a programme of constant, consistent and daily practice, here meaning some study each day as close to seven days per week as possible, the capacity to become capable of communicating with good effect in Italian is certainly possible. Not what anyone would regard as being full fluency, but offering the possibility of reaching a level of competence with spoken Italian that will enable a serious student to speak and converse with confidence.

For the purposes of this discussion, I am defining the term 'partially fluent' in the following terms:

Someone who has achieved a level of Italian that enables them to carry out most of the everyday functions needed when living or moving around Italy over a short or longer period.

They should be capable of renting a car, apartment or booking into a local hotel, ordering and paying for a meal, booking air or train tickets, doing the daily shopping, negotiating and generally capable of taking part in a face-to-face conversation with a native Italian, albeit a relatively slow one. (Slow here meaning the student's level of conversation and definitely not the native Italian!!)

This may sound a lot, but you will be pleasantly surprised to find that by the use of some of the following suggested means to achieving such a level of competence in Italian, success is most definitely within the realms of the possible. Not only is it possible but also within a reasonable amount of time, requiring considerably less than the minimum 10,000 hours of study referred to earlier. I will expand more on the time aspect of advanced learning a little later.

A guide to learning Italian

What follows is a guide to learning Italian with a difference. It also contains some important to know general information about Italy the country, a little about Italians too, plus a brief discussion on how what is known as Standard Italian came about in the first place.

The latter subject does not mean that you should expect to be burdened with a few chapters of boring history. Just a short review detailing how Standard Italian evolved.

For good measure I have also included, for those readers who may be interested, a description of what to my mind is one of Italy's more interesting regions, the northern province of Treviso.

This is a province of many contrasts. It also contains the ancient city of Treviso – the destination I chose for my journey to prove if my programme of advanced language learning had been able to achieve what I had set out to do.

It is also important to note that I have deliberately referred to the end result of becoming a 'proficient (capable) speaker' of Italian, a level I would expect to be achieved as a result of what I will later discuss as a programme of 'self-tuition'.

I, for example, have no illusions of being able to reach full fluency in Italian. Nor do I believe full fluency to be an absolute necessity for the purpose of becoming capable of moving around Italy, contributing to and most importantly – being able to add considerably to the enjoyment of either a short or extended visit to the country.

As a native English speaker, I originally had fond hopes of becoming capable of conversing fluently in Italian. That desirable state may well eventuate with the passing of time and with more continuing study and practice on my part. That status however, I am afraid for all practical purposes is reserved for those among us who are lucky, keen or desperate enough to want to spend at least a full year, preferably two or even more living close to or with an Italian family, while working or studying in Italy.

Fluency in any language can only come about with regular daily use and interaction with the people living in the country. While someone being a native English speaker may feel they can reach that stage, it is a large step from being what I would describe here as becoming a proficient communicator in Italian, to actually becoming one of the near-native Italian-speaking variety.

So, let's not get too bogged down on this as an issue even before we really get started…

Most people met with during my studies and the writing of this book, when questioned on what were their realistic learning expectations, stated that their main desire was to become capable of doing most of the things necessary during either of a long or short stay in Italy. That means, for all practical purposes, being able to converse with a degree of freedom, not necessarily possessing the fluency of a native speaker, but enough to be capable of listening to an Italian, comprehending what it is that they are saying, then being capable of replying and conversing with them with a reasonable degree of speed clarity and confidence.

Having cleared this up at the start now allows me to get down a little later to providing some guidelines on the selection and use of some of the more valuable aids to language learning, useful information for anyone who may be contemplating a similar level of proficiency in spoken Italian.

Obstacles (blockers) mean situations that most adult second language students will find themselves coming up against from time to time. Situations that will occur to many and may deter some native English speakers trying desperately to achieve at least some level of fluency, but find that without the possibility to spend a great deal of time living in Italy makes the task more difficult, some might even say impossible!

The latter statement, one often heard and which I seriously considered myself from time to time during my own journey, is a reasonable comment to make. Thoughts like these may well have occurred to any adult student of Italian, unable to afford either the time or expense involved with becoming fully involved with Italy and its culture. The lack of either the time to be able to study or lack of money of course will make the task of learning any second language that much harder, particularly if trying to advance much beyond the earlier stages of the learning process.

I do not subscribe to some of the more negative views occasionally being offered up as an excuse for a student eventually giving up on their learning programme. Having proved to myself following my own journey, that with a positive approach to the subject, hard work plus a degree of self-belief, becoming able to communicate well enough to be clearly understood in Italian is not only possible, it is a real and worthy goal to aim for. It might take a little time to achieve, but it is certainly possible.

Consider three regularly posed questions:

- "Is it possible to surmount most of the barriers that are known confront anyone in the process of learning a second language, without having the luxury of being able to reside for a long period in Italy?"

  I would like to think that the answer to that question is a definite yes.

- "Is it realistic to claim, like some purveyors of Italian language courses do – that it is possible to learn to speak Italian within a month or so, some claim even less, without the need to be living in the country?"

  I do not believe it possible – unless of course we are to define the ability to speak Italian as the gaining of a few, short, often badly pronounced Italian phrases. Unfortunately, such a claim can often be seen in advertisements for some Italian courses and tutoring services.

- "What steps can a student of Italian, living in Australia or some other English speaking country, take to become a reasonably proficient Italian speaker. If this is not able to be achieved as quickly as some of the more aggressive sellers of language teaching services claim, what is realistic when it comes to the time and effort involved?"

For my views on this, please read on…

It's like hitting up against a wall

Hitting up against a seemingly immovable wall is a stage that both I and, I believe, most other adult English-speaking students of Italian will experience at some time or another during their journey.

By this I mean the point at which, once having gained a broad knowledge of Italian verbs and an understanding of how to use their various forms, they (students) should by then have gained a good understanding of Italian grammar. They should also have acquired a better understanding of some of the fundamental differences between Italian and English. Hopefully also, they will have found themselves in possession of a fairly broad range of Italian vocabulary and expressions.

Moving beyond that point, however, most will eventually get to experience difficulty. This will usually occur at a time when they eventually find themselves confronted with the need to put everything learned thus far into practice. They have now reached a stage in their studies when they wish to hold an intelligent face-to-face conversation in Italian.

That point may also be described as a time when most students will find themselves much in the same place as a long distance runner – someone needing to extend themselves physically beyond a given point in their current capacity to run faster, further or for longer. They have reached a point at which they find themselves hitting up against what seems to be a wall – a seemingly immovable barrier, both physical and mental.

In reality, the wall one hits along the way when it comes to learning a second language is a little different to the one a runner hits. It certainly presents as a mental one. This is a situation where, even if one possesses a reasonably broad range of vocabulary and has learned and absorbed a range of verbs while understanding how they are intended to fit together, there remains a further stage to be traversed.

In an attempt to break through that wall, my search led me to try a variety of Internet-based Italian language services and aids.

Some of these services were available at little or no cost, others at varying cost levels, depending on the extent and scope of the service being offered. I also sourced a selection of available Italian grammar publications. More importantly perhaps, my search and later negative experiences with some of the services and learning aids I tried required me to undertake regular reviews of my progress. This meant assessing how some of the services I trialled were capable of fitting into the programme I was seeking to develop.

The self-study programme that finally emerged was based around a few of the aids I had I found to be the most helpful to my quest. As a result, I was able to construct a regular programme of studies using them. One important principle that applied when selecting a service or learning aid, was that it had to be capable of being fitted into a study programme built around the time I had available, outside then business and other commitments.

In other words, I found it possible to devise a process of learning that was capable of taking me around, through or over the barrier I had found myself coming up against, and which could be comfortably woven into my other time commitments.

The flexibility gained, while requiring me to set aside sufficient time to gain maximum benefit from the programme, later enabled me to progress further toward a higher level of understanding and improved language retention.

The programme of study that finally emerged and then became set into my daily routine eventually enabled me, with some understandable limitations when it came to the level of fluency I was able to achieve, to gain sufficient vocabulary and confidence with its use as to enable me to progress much further toward my goal.

Why study Italian in the first place?

Why indeed? The title of this book is a reasonable question to ask. It is one that I have often asked myself and believe useful to discuss further.

When considering the question from an Australian or any other adult English speakers' position, one answer I came across recently was offered on its website by South Australia's Flinders University.

This Internet site, as part of the description of courses in Italian being offered by the university, discussed how the Italian language and culture had and continues to serve to change and influence not only the way of life and living in South Australia, but by implication that of Australia.

In addition to the university's views, it has been acknowledged over the years that Italy and Italians have contributed much toward Australia's development and present-day character. This university's offering on the subject is therefore considered of some interest, particularly when seeking an answer to the question.

A quick 'Google' on the Internet will uncover many more answers to this question, but for brevity I believe the following will serve to provide a good cross-section of comments and opinions. I have included some of the university's comments as they go some way toward confirming that there really does exist a connection between two countries located half the world apart, which continue to have much in common.

In the case of Australia, this includes the view that the very nature of the country has been changed in a number of positive ways by the many Italians who have made Australia their home, more noticeably during the latter half of the 20th century.

Italy is one of the richest cultural repositories to have emerged within Western civilisation. Setting aside the Roman era, since the early Middle Ages Italy has been a world leader in many fields. The first university in Europe was founded in Bologna in 1290. Its School of Law was also a first and is said to have attracted many scholars from across Europe. It is also said that banking and accountancy systems were invented in Italy during the late Middle Ages.

Italy is considered one of the wealthier nations of the world, although to read reports on the nation's financial situation nationally at any given time would seem to place some doubt on this. Nevertheless, Italy has also become an essential international destination, being visited regularly by tourists, students and scholars from all corners of the known world.

It is also interesting to record here that over recent years there has been much evidence to suggest that more and more Italian tourists, particularly younger Italians, are seeking to visit, and in a number of cases to work and possibly resettle in Australia.

Italian, after English, is reputed to be the most widely spoken language in Australia, with over half a million Australians of Italian extraction and connections using the language in one form or another every day. It is also said that you can practice and put Italian to use in any number of Australian communities.

You can also apparently, according to the university, virtually live 'Italian-style' in South Australia. I am not sure what the university meant by that, but like other regions across the country, many first and second generation Italians are known to continue to follow and maintain much of the culture that their forebears brought with them to Australia.

Italian, the university site also commented, "can prove to be a pathway to employment". As well, it said that Italy is a major trading partner with Australia, increasingly so with South Australia, with knowledge of Italian seen by the university to be of some benefit in such fields as tourism, music, design, architecture, teaching, technology, science and commerce.

The first Italian in South Australia is said to have arrived in the then British colony in 1839. Since then, South Australian citizens of Italian origin have made innumerable contributions to the development of the State.

* * *

Comment

A similar claim to that above can also be applied to other states across Australia. Not only is Italy and its long history owned by Europe, it is expected to continue to remain an important source of inspiration and continuing interest and affection for many Australians.

* * *

Another good reason to study Italian

From time to time we read opinions being issued from various scientific and medical organisations, some to the effect that mentally stimulating Internet and other games designed to exercise our minds, may well be of long-term benefit to our ongoing mental health. This view is seen to be particularly important when discussing problems that some people experience trying to hold off the potential onset of mental deterioration, particularly so during the later years of life. This kind of unwanted development is thus considered worthy of comment here.

While Flinders University provides a reasonably acceptable answer to the question of "why study Italian?" the mental stimulation that is known to result from learning a second language perhaps bears a little more weight. This is particularly so when it comes to the question of what kind of strategy one should try to adopt to maintain mental health during our latter years

An opinion on this subject was reported recently in *The Telegraph* newspaper of London, where it was claimed that a study carried out by a team of researchers from the University of Edinburgh, found that: "Bilingual people are twice as likely to recover from a stroke than those who speak only one language".

The same team was also reported to have previously postulated that bilingual people were expected to be able to delay the onset of dementia some several years later on average, than mono-linguists.

Researchers from the university also reported that a later study suggested that the challenge involved with learning to speak in a language other than their own could boost what is termed as the brain's 'cognitive reserve' – in other words, its capacity to cope with damage.

A recent study published by Tasmanian researchers, reported in the Melbourne *Age* of November 21st 2015, found that older adults who decide to take up a challenging college course, might find one advantage of doing so their being able to look forward to a reduction in their risk of suffering the early onset of dementia.

In that study, more than 300 over-50s were followed for three years as they took part in full or part-time courses in history, psychology, philosophy and fine arts at the University of Tasmania. More than 90% of the survey's participants as a result displayed a significant increase in cognitive capacity, compared with 56% of a control group who took no classes.

So there you have it, whether we choose to accept the findings of the universities referred to here, and there may well be other studies with findings along similar lines, there would appear to be at least two strong cases in support of embarking upon the usually mentally stimulating challenge of intensive study.

Simply taking up the study of something challenging may well be part of the answer to a mental health problem that health authorities around the Western world are expecting to be faced by an increasing number of people, particularly among those more elderly within their populations.

It would also seem to follow that there are a number of other advantages to be gained intellectually, simply by taking up the study of a second language.

A summary of three reports discussing research into the advantages of taking on the learning of a second language, and how long it will take, are included in the References section.

3. Thinking in Italian

The potentially debilitating onset of mental deterioration during our latter years aside, the need to learn how to think more efficiently in Italian might sound just a little confronting to an English speaker taking up the study of the language. At first it can be.

Consider what is involved when trying to adapt oneself, particularly if an adult, toward mastering a second language – in this case a language other than the one you have spoken for most of your life to date?

When you really come to think more deeply about the need to become able to think more efficiently in Italian to eventually speak with greater clarity when using the language, the process involved can and often does appear intimidating. This can be particularly so when any long-time English speaker decides to set their sights on achieving a more advanced level of usable proficiency in Italian.

Part-time adult students should expect that at some point during their study programme that they will eventually arrive at a point, usually around or just beyond intermediate level, where they will begin to find difficulty making progress. Difficulties with moving much further beyond that stage are most likely to appear at or near the time when they begin to feel sufficiently advanced in their studies to now be able to engage in an actual conversation in Italian.

It is here when they will find themselves limited when they try to communicate, using their recently acquired stock of Italian words and phrases.

Most will begin to find that there are skills, other than just the learning of Italian grammar and the gathering of vocabulary that is required, if they are to improve their capacity, particularly when trying to put together a coherent conversation. This will become even clearer when they try to transition smoothly from their natural English tongue, to the one with which they wish to communicate.

I have come to know that difficulty, once a student has gained a good grasp of grammar, verbs etc., as now needing to develop the capacity to be able to *think* more in an Italian way. At least to become more capable of forming thoughts in Italian, as opposed to their usual, familiar and comfortable English.

To put the problem another way, the need now becomes one of embracing the idiomatic or colloquial use of Italian words, phrases and speech patterns, the language form as used naturally in their everyday lives by native Italians. This, together with the need to become more familiar with the way words and phrases need to be put together when structuring a conversation in Italian – a way of communicating (speaking) very different to English in a number of important ways.

Understand the problem this way… In my case, my native language is English. English is the only language I learned from childhood. All my dreams are dreamed in English and all my thoughts are and have always been generated in English. How I express those thoughts also emerges using a recognisable form of English idiom, one that relates closely to the city, town and part of England where I was born and where I first learned how to speak. For me, this was the county of Yorkshire in England's north.

Even following over fifty years' residence in Australia, I still retain a distinct Yorkshire accent, as well as the remnants of a northern English turn of phrase. My natural mode of speech to this day is one that even serves to differentiate me from other English speakers, born and raised in other parts of the United Kingdom, or anywhere else in the English-speaking world. I have also found that Italians trying to cope with the English language sometimes find it difficult to follow my turn of phrase, particularly if I happen to be speaking at my normal rate of knots.

When it comes down to basics, most of us, when trying to learn Italian, whether we are from either of an English, Australian, New Zealand, American or Canadian background will inevitably find ourselves thinking about what it is that we wish to say primarily in the way we would express ourselves in our natural English idiom that we carry from childhood.

This process will automatically occur before we try to convert the content of what it is we want to communicate, now needing to express this in an Italian idiom – in an Italian's way of using language.

Now the task becomes one of trying to convert our natural way of thinking into the language we are trying to master.

If you really think about it, early on in the study of our desired second language, it becomes inevitable that whenever we try to put more than a couple of Italian words, a phrase, and certainly a sentence or two together, our first move will be to involuntarily think about what it is we wish to say, but in English.

Having decided on this, we will then try to translate our English thoughts into Italian words, usually in a form that appears to be roughly equivalent to similarly meaning Italian words.

At first, we will usually try to achieve this by using a form of English words that we would normally use to describe what it is we wish to say, but translated as best we can into similar or equivalent meaning Italian words.

We will quickly realise however that Italians don't often, if at all, use the same form of words to describe the same thing or situation as we would in English. Not only that, but an Italian's way of describing a given situation is often quite different to the way an English speaker would use words to describe the same situation.

Further on this important point. Anyone who has gone through this process will have realised that while whatever it was that we were thinking of in English might well have made good sense and be readily understood when spoken of in English, it often ceases to emerge as such when delivered in equivalent Italian words. Certainly not in the manner we may have first thought that it should have.

To expand further on this point, not only will we find a problem with being able to translate our English thoughts into a correct turn of phrase in Italian, but we will also find, often to our dismay, that our capacity to put together the necessary words and phrases into a logical Italian-style sequence will evade us.

The inability to use the correct form of Italian will continue to evade us until we have become capable of assembling and absorbing a broader range of Italian vocabulary. Even then, we will still need to have learned how to put the various Italian words needed together – in the correct sequence.

This, in practice, means possession of a broad enough range of Italian words, together with sufficient understanding and confidence with the way they need to be put together. Only then will our level of spoken Italian allow us to express what we wish to say, in a form that would be reasonably close to being correct and able to make some sense to an Italian!

Italians often use a different combination of and possibly a different sequence of words to those a speaker of English would normally use. This is just one aspect of language learning that highlights the often wide differences between how an Italian speaker would be expected to express a thought, phrase or description of a situation that is happening, has happened or that they expect will happen – or perhaps may happen.

Until an English speaker has become capable of switching their brain a little faster into a mode of thinking that could be described as 'Italian', the capacity to move beyond that point in his or her studies will inevitably hit up against a seemingly immovable barrier to their ability to progress much further.

Most adult English-speaking students who are now in the process of learning Italian, indeed any other second language, will have found that it is not possible to gain a practical level of competency in their chosen second language, unless and until they have gained for themselves at least some of the skills necessary to becoming able to switch their thinking over to Italian.

This prerequisite to becoming a proficient speaker is important to understand and work toward. It is not, however, a skill that most will find easy to master.

A short, simple example as to the different manner by which an English speaker would use words to describe something that had occurred to him or her, as opposed to how an Italian would more than likely describe the same situation, serves to demonstrate this point.

I have a cold

Take for example the very simple statement in English "I have caught a cold", or perhaps "I have a cold". Now, you might think to state the same in Italy by using the Italian words *ho un raffredore* – a direct translation of the English. While this phrase would sound correct to an English speaker, it is different to the sequence and meaning of words that an Italian would use to describe the same situation.

Discussing the same phrase, an Italian would more usually be heard to say, *me e venuto un raffredore.* Translated word-for-word directly into English, the Italian words would say "To me has come, (came) a cold".

If an Italian used a direct translation in English of the form of words that he/she would normally use in Italy ("To me has come (came) a cold") to indicate that they had become afflicted with a cold, the phrase would sound odd and not the way one would be expected to describe the situation in English. This is why the form of words an Italian visitor to Australia or any other English-speaking country would use will often sound strange to an English speakers' ear, their way of speaking alone instantly defining them as being foreign.

The reverse of course will also apply in the case of a native English speaker trying to communicate in Italian.

There are many such examples of differences between the way in which the English and Italian languages flow, others more complex than the simple example provided. This one example should, however, serve to explain just one of many areas of Italian requiring closer study and understanding, before any student of Italian can get closer to mastering the spoken or written language.

It bears repeating here that 'it's the way in which an Italian would say or describe something', more often than not in a much different form to that which would be used by an English speaker attempting to describe a similar activity or thought.

Trying to gain the skills required to advance to a point of becoming capable of translating English style thinking across to Italian, cannot be gained by continued reliance solely on the usual form of relatively static, mainly book based classroom style tuition, the kind of learning environment provided by most established language schools.

The capacity to advance will, however, improve if augmented by the use of an effective range of learning aids and practical exercises. This is, always, provided that students understand the need to extend their learning experience beyond the classroom and along a different study routine.

This will mean working toward gaining the necessary language and thinking skills on a daily basis, – along with personal discipline and commitment – while using an appropriate range of learning aids.

Comment

Developing the capacity to switch or adapt your way of thinking toward the way an Italian would express himself or herself is a vital step in the process toward gaining the capacity to converse effectively in Italian.

* * *

Living in Italy over a long period while being exposed to the language and everyday way of living among its inhabitants, will eventually permeate most adult students' minds and eventually enable them to communicate much earlier in their adopted language.

Being for the most part adult part-time students, when added to the obvious drawback of living far away from Italy, students of Italian living in Australia or anywhere else in the English-speaking world will find learning to think more in an Italian way harder to achieve. Accepting this obvious limitation, however, by the addition of a year or so of self-tuition, coupled to the use of the learning aids and exercises to be discussed later, will offer a serious student of Italian a different, creative and, I believe, more economic route by which to overcome many of the barriers to thinking more effectively in Italian.

The means to achieving success as defined earlier, are readily available to those motivated and prepared to work hard enough toward gaining the necessary skills…

More about learning to think in Italian

Most established schools and other marketers of language courses being offered these days appear to assume that the more one studies and reads Italian texts, then it should follow that becoming capable of conversing in Italian will eventually happen. Often, little emphasis is placed on the important and yet regularly ignored element of tuition needed to assist a student to become better able to think more easily and smoothly, Italian-style.

This more advanced element of language learning, once having gained the basic elements of grammar and word structure, should then form an important part of every student's ongoing learning processes, now having reached what is generally regarded as an 'intermediate' stage in their studies – a kind of 'halfway-house' if you like.

One Internet service offering actually makes the statement "Think like an Italian, speak like an Italian". The same site later goes on to discuss this important aspect of the learning process by suggesting to potential clients that they should "Forget your native tongue" and "If you want to speak Italian, then spend some time in Italy speaking only Italian".

Statements like these, while they sound eminently sensible and straight forward, are unhelpful. Bear in mind that what they state is precisely that which every student would like very much to achieve – if only they knew how! The same website later followed their earlier statements with the comment "If you want to read Italian, then pick up an Italian newspaper and peruse whatever section interests you". Once again, that statement also refers to a skill that all would like to be capable of doing, if only they could.

The presumed point of the above exhortations, once distilled a little, seem intended to communicate the message: "To achieve competency in Italian you must aim at being able to think and speak like an Italian", which of course is absolutely true!

The foregoing, we might observe if using the Australian vernacular, are statements of the 'bloody obvious'. That particular site does offer a number of important points to be kept in mind when trying to learn Italian:

> Learning scripted responses in foreign languages encourages a false sense of confidence. It doesn't translate into real-time speaking competence nor will you understand the musicality of the language. It's like looking at a musical score and expecting to be a master violinist just because you have memorised the notes. Instead you have to play it, and play it again and again. Likewise with the Italian language.
>
> Play with it! Practice! Listen to native Italian speakers and mimic them. Laugh at yourself trying to pronounce "gli" correctly. Italian, more so than many languages, is musical, and if you remember that analogy it will come easier.
>
> There is no secret, no Rosetta Stone, no silver bullet when it comes to learning a language. You have to listen and repeat ad nauseam. You will make a quantum leap in learning Italian when you abandon your native tongue and disengage from the grammar that you implicitly learned when you were a child.

The question here that really needs to be answered is:

What does one need do to learn to think more easily in Italian?

Learning to think in Italian, while a difficult step for most native English speakers, might well be less of a problem for a current native speaker of another of the so-called group of 'Romance' languages, French or Spanish.

The fact is that most English speakers, certainly those of us wishing to gain some competence in Italian, do not have the possibility of living in Italy for a prolonged period. Even if we did eventually get to travel and stay in the country for a while, it would be far better for our eventual success if we were to equip ourselves a little better when it comes to learning to think better in an Italian way, before commencing any planned stay in the country.

It is one thing to write that a student needs to be capable of thinking more in Italian, but how to go about that difficult transition is something altogether different. The need to place much more emphasis on trying to develop a deeper appreciation for the 'rhythm' by which the language flows is also important.

I came to realise that much was to be gained during the learning process if, having arrived at a point where I had gained a reasonable level of familiarity with the general structure of Italian verbs and grammar, and had managed to gather a sufficiently broad range of vocabulary, it now became important to switch emphasis.

Past experience had also shown that few, if any of the companies marketing their various styles of language courses, and most of the teaching staff employed at the schools I had attended, appeared capable (perhaps they were uncommitted or not really interested) when it came to delivering all that most had been claiming via their advertising and publicity. What was their actual success rate, as against that which they claimed? I often used to wonder.

How many of them are really successful, particularly when it comes to the number of their students actually gaining the capacity to speak well in Italian? The most I was able to gain on inquiry were the kind of endorsements being used in advertisements, all presumably donated by (friendly) past students, none of which represented a realistic indication of the level of success both they and their systems of language education had achieved.

From my experiences as a student, and comments received from other past students of various schools, it seems likely that only a small percentage of those who start with the aim of becoming a proficient speaker of Italian actually go on to succeed at the level they had originally set out to.

At best, all that any adult student should expect from a part-time classroom-based language-teaching course is to be able to gain a firm basis of grammar and some additional capacity when it comes to reading. Such courses are not really equipped to provide a student with all that is required to advance themselves much beyond that point. Attendance at a classroom-based course for one or perhaps two occasions each week over a relatively long period can also be excessively expensive as well as being incapable of producing confident speakers.

For me, therefore, the answer now was to look beyond the usual crop of school-based courses on offer and more toward the use of a selection of language services and aids different to the limited few I had become used to using thus far. That meant scouring the Internet in search of a range of learning aids capable of being incorporated into an ongoing programme of self-study, including practical exercises, which I intended to work with outside the usual format of a school classroom.

Following location and evaluation of Internet-based services and aids thought to be appropriate, I then worked toward the formulation of a daily schedule of study and practical exercises that I hoped would be able to take me toward my goal.

Note here that I had determined on the need for as close to a daily study and practice schedule possible, organised as best I could to align with my other commitments.

Did you try studying French in school?

How many of us, during long-since-completed primary and secondary school years, in which we were perhaps inflicted with a year or two of French, German or even Japanese or Chinese, went on to harbour the thought later during our adulthood, that it would be fun trying to become proficient in a second language?

I don't know about you, but thinking back to my early school days, just the effort of wrestling with English grammar at the time was enough to put me off trying to come to grips with a second language. Of course in those days, having had a few prior years' practice with thinking in English, as well since babyhood having learned to speak with reasonable clarity, made the eventual learning of English grammar far easier than my struggles with Italian grammar were proving, many years later.

Here I am thinking more along the lines of having eventually made it to adulthood, then having travelled a few times to one or two of the more exotic and interesting vacationing spots around the globe. Destinations like Europe, Russia, Japan, Indonesia, Southeast Asia, North or South America etc. Perhaps also during one or other such a trip, the idea of learning a language other than your native English may well have grabbed your attention as being a good idea at the time?

No? Well, even if you haven't experienced that particular desire, or have yet to become afflicted with the need to take up the study of a second language as an adult, please read on. What I will be discussing later, particularly when it comes to a potentially better way to achieving proficiency in Italian, might just fire up your interest to learn a second language!

When it came to Asian languages, I had little interest to travel extensively in the Asian region, so I discarded that idea quite early. Even the thought of trying to come to grips with complex Japanese or Chinese characters, a task that seems enough to put off some native citizens of those countries, also left me more than a little disinterested.

One or other of the European languages shouldn't be that all that difficult to learn, should they?

Don't most of them use the same or similar letters and numerals as we in Australia and other countries having English as their main or national language? OK, perhaps we need to forget the Cyrillic style of lettering as used in Slavic languages and Russian, and the Greek alphabet. But surely French, Italian – or even German, perhaps, should prove simple enough to get one's English-oriented tongue around?

Many English speakers, other than folks like me who, having descended from grandparents who spoke German, or to be more exact Yiddish,[2] would be expected to find pronouncing

---

[2] "Yiddish (*yidish/idish*), literally 'Jewish', in older sources 'Yiddish-Taitsh' (English: *Judaeo-German*), is the historical language of the Ashkenazi Jews. It originated during the 9th century in Central Europe, providing the nascent Ashkenazi community with an extensive Germanic based vernacular ... Yiddish is written with a fully vocalized alphabet based on the Hebrew script." (Source: *Wikipedia*.)

words using the guttural sounding consonant *ch* in words like *ach, tochter, rauch, buch* etc. more than a little challenging.

In any case, as you may perhaps be planning at some stage to visit Rome, the Amalfi coast, Tuscany, Venice, Sicily or some other holiday location in Italy in the future, why not try learning a little Italian? It is after all a melodious and romantic language and one that uses an alphabet similar, but not exactly the same as English.

Language – The expression of a country's soul

How many non-Italians have become caught in the thrall of that beautiful and historically important country?

I guess any discussion around things Italian could apply to any number of Italy's unique features, not the least being its friendly, open and sometimes excitable people. Italy is also the home of some of the world's most successful football teams. It is also the source of a mouth-watering array of exquisite wines and food, and possessor of a unique culture that has given the world some of its more renowned writers, singers, artists, scientists and astronomers. Visiting Italy for the first time is to discover a unique combination of history and culture, its capital Rome also playing a historical role, that of being the central focus of the Roman Catholic Church, one of the world's major religions.

Knowing at least something of Italy's long, turbulent history, while trying to fathom what makes its often difficult to follow political system tick, how many of us have at one time or other found ourselves succumbing to the thought that we might just indulge ourselves a little deeper in things Italian? Some may even have harboured thoughts of becoming a proficient speaker of its language.

For a citizen of a country not having an overly strong Latin base as the underlying foundation of its language, becoming familiar with Latin-based Italian will be understandably a little more difficult. With so many providers of Italian language learning programmes on offer however, one or two of the more questionable promising to be capable of teaching anyone to speak Italian from the first lesson, the possibility of becoming reasonably proficient in the language shouldn't be all that difficult?

How satisfying would it be to find oneself capable of ordering a meal or reserving a hotel room in Italian? To also experience joy at being able to haggle with a local shopkeeper or stallholder and having the reasonable expectation of being successful at gaining a *sconto* (discount) on the price of a luxuriously tooled leather bag, printed silk scarf or belted leather jacket?

Being able and confident when it comes to the need to ask a passer-by for directions could also be a great way of adding more enjoyment to any visit to Italy, as would making that long-dreamed-of visit to St Peter's Basilica or any one of many other of Italy's more popular vacation sites, in a country virtually overflowing with them.

4. Alice in Wonderland

Italy and its people throughout history have played their part in the world, mainly as a result of human migrations from practically every region, city or town. Similar regular movements of people have over the years served to carry Italian traditions, its culture, language and cuisine to many new homelands.

Australia is one country that over a number of years before and two decades following the ending of the Second World War saw a complete change in the mix and size of its population.

Waves of immigrants following the end of that war, including Italian, Austrian, Polish, Dutch, German, Greek and Turkish migrants decided to leave a struggling post-war Europe, in large numbers, many making for an Australia that was then a still young and relatively empty continent. All were in addition to many thousands of newcomers to Australia who arrived there from the British Isles.

Later migrations of Vietnamese, Chinese, Indian, Afghan and Sri Lankan refugees also became part of the Australian population mix, particularly during years following the 1940s and 1950s. Many even earlier migrations of Chinese and Afghans had already established themselves in the country, most during the earlier gold-rush days of the 19th century.

In addition to the eating and drinking habits of an earlier more languid, relatively small and almost exclusively British population that peopled the vast Australian continent between the two major wars, Australia has become a country no longer British in its makeup, outlook, or cuisine.

Over the decades since 1945, the country has become a truly cosmopolitan Commonwealth of Australia. It is true also to note here that Italy and Italians have played a considerable role in that transformation.

Excited anticipation

It is often too easy when arriving in Italy, for a first-time visitor to find him or herself being carried away with the heady romance of just being in a country that is so different in so many ways to the country, city or town in which they are a permanent resident.

Visiting Italy on vacation, the usual way most visitors get to begin their connection with the country, can sometimes be likened to a relatively new visitor becoming temporarily overpowered by a mild but pleasant form of what you might call 'sensual intoxication.'

Now don't get me wrong here, I am in no way comparing any of the emotions usually felt on being a new visitor to Italy with the overuse of alcohol or any other of the known drugs and other forms of intoxicant that may be imbibed, smoked, snorted, or injected. Not at all!

During a visit to Italy, more particularly perhaps in the case of a traveller landing there for the first time, much like I was during the early 1970s, some people have even been known to feel themselves to be in the midst of a mild form of rapture. By this I mean a first-time traveller finding him or herself in what may be described as something similar to delight, or perhaps a state more elegantly described as an 'elevated state of excited anticipation'? Something akin to them entering a kind of 'Alice in Wonderland'–like scenario, the wonderland in this case being Italy and the traveller in the form of Alice. I recall that my first visit had me experiencing similar feelings of excitement and anticipation.

The Alice in Wonderland analogy may not be all that far from reality when experiencing some of Italy's customs and way of doing things for the first time, sometimes amusing also frustrating situations that will often occur during the short period usually spent in Italy by most first-time visitors. They will of course encounter situations that may also find them endeavouring to cope with the excessive speed and often overly flamboyant driving habits of Italian drivers, particularly the male variety.

First-time visitors to Italy are often surprised to find most of the local shops closing their doors for what to most westerners would appear to be an excessively elongated lunchtime break. Trying to make their way through a crowd of fellow tourists thronging the most popular Italian tourist venues, particularly during the summer months, can also serve to turn even a short visit into an annoying and tiring scramble.

One of the pastimes I enjoy when visiting Italy is to observe and listen in to conversations among visitors who happen to be travelling in the same places I am.

Sometimes I may even get to assist in situations where, even with my as yet imperfect Italian, I have found myself able to assist other visitors who may be sitting in the same restaurant, struggling perhaps as they endeavour to puzzle their way through a menu presented entirely in Italian.

In a very different situation, it can sometimes be amusing observing non-Italian-speaking visitors standing on a railway platform as they await their connection to another city, let's say for example – Florence. For most, being unable to understand the loudspeaker announcement echoing along the platform can prove to be very inconvenient. It (the loudspeaker) may well be telling the gathered throng that the train to Florence they were expecting to arrive alongside platform #4, at the time originally indicated on the railway station's digital noticeboards, will not now be arriving there. Instead it will now be thirty minutes late and will arrive instead at platform #7!

Foreign visitors in such a situation are rather easy to identify, as the rest of those waiting alongside them take off with a run toward the newly advised platform, leaving any remaining foreign visitors standing there confused and disoriented.

Many books have been written about life in Italy and the many different facets of Italian life as experienced by their writers.

Some writers tend to wax lyrical about their Italian experiences, while others present a perhaps more critical picture of their time spent somewhere in the country. Still others talk generally about the glamour of the women and the dash and sometimes-overt sexuality of the men. You know, the earlier famed historical propensity of male Italians when it came to bottom pinching, a practice that we often used to hear a lot about, something these days that has rightly come to be regarded as a criminal assault, and as such frowned upon by most of the Italian community.

Some travellers have written about perceived shortcomings,

when recording their views on the style of Italian public life. It is often difficult to follow the processes of Italian government and the day-by-machinations of the various political parties and their internal factions. Their cartoonlike leaders are often being pursued and accused of a variety of misdemeanours that in any other democratically run country would have long since found them 'banged up' in a state penitentiary, or banished to obscurity.

In Italy such characters are generally accepted by many among the long-suffering populace, sometimes with a resigned shrug of the shoulders and a comment along the lines of "What do you expect? They are politicians."

The following References section, in addition to information on Italian courses and learning aids, suggests just two of a number of books written in English that a new visitor to Italy would find useful to pick up and read before travelling. Both writers featured delve a little deeper into what makes Italy and the Italian way of thinking and doing things so different to the way other nationalities go about living their lives.

There are many other books to choose from. I have included the two recommended, one written by an English academic, a long-time resident in Italy, the other a native Italian. They both provide an interesting view of what any new visitor to the country should expect to meet up with during their travels.

Italian media

Should you happen to eventually find yourself in Italy, turning on the TV in your hotel room can prove to be an interesting experience. Unfortunately most local hotels, particularly those located in smaller, provincial cities and towns, have their TVs tuned only to receive Italian-speaking stations. In such a situation, it is either a case of just watching the pictures or trying to pick up the gist of what is being reported or discussed. If interested in sport, it is possible to follow a football or rugby match without the benefit of understanding the usually excitable, rapid and voluble explanations on the state of play offered by the local commentator.

Your TV screen, on logging onto any one of the local stations, will more than likely be liberally sprinkled with a dawn to dark parade of short-skirted, often provocatively gowned, predominantly blond women, both young and not so young. Many, from their appearance on screen could have you believing that they are intent on entering a Miss or Mrs Italy Sexy-lady competition!

I have yet to see a matching array of plunging necklines, tantalising and sometimes revealing thigh length skirts and well-developed, provocatively presented and often openly displayed bosoms being featured on Australian TV screens, and certainly not on the even more staid BBC.

TV programming in Italy can be very different to the way in which serious programmes are presented in the US, Australia, Britain and other Western countries. In Italy, your TV viewing might even be brightened up with the sight of one or perhaps two glamorous gals hosting or running a talk show. Some of these programmes turn out to be a serious discussion on a current affairs subject or something equally serious in nature.

Shows like these are sometimes led by a fast-talking, more often than not 'busty' female facilitator, precariously balancing on a pair of trim, extra long slim legs. Usually with this kind of show, the female presenter or assistant, if partnering a male, will be positioned so that her physical attributes can be displayed in the most effective way possible. On the end of a lovely pair of legs being so displayed, are more than likely to be found feet encased in the highest heeled pair of designer shoes she could find, from among one or other of the high fashion boutiques of Rome and Milan.

Mind you, most of these female anchors and discussion leaders are usually well capable of matching the ability of their male companions, both in their assertiveness and subject knowledge. This, when added to their sometimes-overt sexiness and dress makes their presence compelling and perhaps a little confronting for some male viewers.

Italian TV offers a myriad of stations, a range catering for every possible taste imaginable. Some of these stations will also be sprinkled with more than the usual number of programmes of a distinctly religious nature. Be it known that throughout Italy the Pope, the titular head of the Roman Catholic Church, is regarded as having superstar status, with local TV stations and news bulletins following his every move and pronouncement with respectful deference and reverence.

In contrast, product advertising on Italian TV will often feature a sexily clad female who may well be trying to interest the viewing public in what seems, on the surface, to be a boring product or household accessory. Or, you could find yourself enchanted to see a gorgeously attired sex siren draped suggestively across a relatively uninteresting sponge rubber mattress covered in printed cotton, stroking it as her facial expressions appear to offer delightful experiences to come…

Others can regularly be observed draped variously and suggestively over a chair or couch, while the voiceover drones on in rapid-fire Italian, describing the technicalities or advantages of what is being portrayed on screen (about the product unfortunately – not the girl).

On the other side of the coin, in contrast to such overt sexuality in advertising, on my last visit to Italy in 2015 one evening I found myself sitting through a TV advertisement in which a young, petite and attractive woman, clad in what looked like the medieval era, full (definitely unrevealing) renaissance dress and headgear. She, the model and presenter in this case seemed intent on interesting the viewing audience in the advantages of possessing the portable shower recess that the accompanying rapid-fire commentary was in the process of rattling on about. The product was a relatively dull piece of basic plumbing that could, we were told, be installed in place of an old bath.

Whichever ad agency creative director had thought up that style of advertisement and the overly sober dressing of the female talent, seemed to this writer at least to have got the historical period and the product they were trying to advertise a bit mixed up. But who knows, to Italian eyes the impression that emerged on the TV screen was obviously thought to work effectively!

The Italian way

Italy often presents as being something of a paradox. A contradiction and an often distracting while amusing place, where a visitor can often find that they are being beguiled and shocked, exasperated and amazed, sometimes simultaneously.

Visitors may also find themselves more than a little confused while trying to understand the various rules, laws, signs, notices and of course not forgetting here them trying to understand the meaning of often lengthy and usually difficult to interpret announcements echoing along a railway station platform.

Italy can be all those things at one time or another. The secret here though is that in spite of some of the more seemingly outrageous performances that you may see portrayed on your hotel's TV screen, or happening among the nation's political establishments, is not to take the place too seriously.

Seek to enjoy your stay whenever you decide to visit and importantly, try also to drink in the atmosphere, antiquity, creativity, modernity, and at times even the serenity of the place in which you find yourself that day. Try not to be put off too much by what sometimes might seem to be a state of chaos and what often appears to be the flagrant use of female sex appeal that you will be confronted with from time to time on Italian television.

If you are an intending new traveller to Italy, it will also pay to read up a little on the country in addition to learning at least something of the language, preferably before undertaking your visit.

Don't try to make too much sense of Italy's sometimes seemingly Keystone Cops–like political system, or the antics, outrageous statements and alleged activities of some of its recent, over-the-top leaders.

Try entering into your travel programme with the understanding that in Italy, nearly every major decision or activity, whether public or private, is often conducted in the form of an operatic performance. Public Italian life sometimes really does seem like finding oneself in the midst of an everyday living, vocal opera, where raised voices do not necessarily mean that a more violent confrontation is in the offing. On the contrary, to speak Italian usually means the use not only of the vocal cords, sometimes at a raised level, but also a speaker's hands – a usual and regular necessity to provide extra in the way of emphasis and colour to any discussion.

With so many aspects of Italian life that can be intriguing to a newcomer, Italy is without any doubt a fabulous country to visit. It is a destination that will reward any visitor, should they take the trouble to try to understand and absorb the style and beat of life there. It can, in fact, be an absorbing pastime to take a mental note of the different ways in which Italians go about doing their 'thing', when compared to other westerners.

Everything about Italy, whether taking in the beauty of much of the countryside, the grandeur of the northern Dolomite mountains and Alps, the innate skills of its artists, glassblowing artists and designers both past and present, or its ancient cities, food, wines and all the other wonderful things there, makes it a place to visit at least once in every person's lifetime.

That certain something...

Now that I have started talking about the citizens of that curiously shaped boot-like peninsula, thrusting itself precociously into the 'middle sea', I should also add that I rapidly came to the view that nearly all Italians, the very young and not so young included, possess what I think is best referred to as 'that certain something'. A certain something, very different to the native culture of most visitors and one that anyone wishing to become proficient in the Italian language should seek to become more familiar with – if they are eventually to achieve success.

Italians have a way of being and doing things that is both

different and special. A way of thinking and living that is so different in so many ways to the manner in which most other westerners go about living their everyday lives.

To most Italians, the way they go about dressing themselves is always of some importance. Dressing in a manner that sees them always aiming to look stylish, often succeeding seemingly without a hitch – even if just in the process of strolling in the piazza or hanging out at a local bar or pizzeria.

Of course, to me, a mere man, Italian women have always appealed, with their innate and uncompromising sense of style and being. Most also seem to possess a very endearing form of coquettishness. A way of just being chic, something that simply being so sets them apart from their perhaps more reserved, less flamboyant British, Nordic and northern European sisters.

Italian women, regardless of their age, always appear to be intent, no matter the time of day or whatever they happen to be doing, in making some kind of statement.

As a keen long-time observer, Italian women, even younger pre-teenage girls, always appear capable without even looking contrived, of making that little dress, skirt or pair of torn jeans, shirt, footwear or designer styled shoulder bag look so very chic. Even in the year just past (2015), during a summer-long and unrelentingly hot July and August, a really sweltering summer that was being felt along the full length of the Italian peninsula. Even during the more uncomfortable days and weeks during that period, the humid weather failed to dampen most Italian women's desire to maintain what I have come to regard as their 'sexy chic' status.

Regardless of a hot sun and sometimes ultra-high humidity, the unfailing desire to be well dressed always seemed capable of maintaining its hold. This often extended to the use of a hand-held fan being waved to and fro as they promenaded down streets and across piazzas, endeavouring wherever possible to maintain at least a breath of air to cool an overheated brow and usually delightfully plunging décolleté.

The passegiata

Being attired fashionably has always been high on the list of things to be aware of being Italian – both male and female. This becomes even more evident on the weekends when, having completed their week of work in the office, shop, factory, school or university, weekends anywhere across the country are usually the time when most Italians will think to take *una passegiata* (a stroll).

Taking a *passegiata* to an Italian, unlike the kind of casual stroll that other westerners may take on a weekend visit to the city or their local park, requires more than just a little in the way of preparation. For one thing, it is usual across Italy for individuals and families undertaking their daily or weekend *passegiata*, to ensure that they are appropriately dressed for the occasion.

Being dressed appropriately becomes more a case of presenting themselves to the world in their best or most stylish, sometimes even outlandish outfit – always depending of course on their age and the image they desire to project, as well as their perceptions as to their social standing.

Italy to my mind is one of the few, possibly the only country in the world where you will regularly see even the very young children of a family happily tagging along with their older siblings, parents and often their grandparents. Families strolling around the local piazza during an afternoon, or more likely later into the evening, particularly during the summer months and school holidays, with the younger children playing among themselves and even taking part in a general *chiacchierare* (conversation or chat) with the rest of their family, cousins and family friends.

The family to most Italians is the central focal point of their relationships. The family, including cousins, uncles, aunts and of course grandparents is the kind of close grouping that a visitor to any part of Italy will usually notice. Notice that is if they care to take the time to look, listen and observe what is going on around them.

This if anything is but one of many ways in which the Italian way of life still continues to revolve around older family members, particularly those in the latter stages of their lives, of whom younger family members will usually show genuine respect for and enduring affection. All this seems to operate in a way that perhaps we in Australia and other Western countries are tending to experience less, as the pressures of a busy life and a differently developing mode of living inexorably serves to force social changes, many perhaps seen by some as not being for the better?

The social changes occurring in other Western societies, gradual though they tend to be, have resulted in a noticeable loosening of what formerly were much closer personal and family inter-relationships. Changes such as these however, appear to be occurring to a lesser extent among Italian families.

What is often described as being the Italian way is really a style of life and pace of daily living that progresses along a much different path to that which I have experienced in Australia, the US and the UK. It is a way of being that often makes life in Australia and most other Western countries in which I have travelled and lived feel different – perhaps less colourful and sometimes lacking a deeper sense of close emotional connections.

Observed differences between any of the various worldwide cultures make it difficult, sometimes a pointless practice trying to make anything like accurate comparisons or valuations – one culture as against another. Trying to make comparisons and judgements between the ways of living as experienced in Australia for example as against those in Italy can prove to be less than helpful, resulting at best in the making of inaccurate and often less than useful comparisons.

Similarly, continuing to reflect personal prejudices without recognising some of the more interesting and meaningful aspects of living through a new experience in a new country, may even threaten a visitor's capacity to enjoy any new experience entered into – their first visit to Italy for example.

Preferences

It is interesting to record some interesting examples of how such perceptions can work, following discussion with younger Italians visiting and working in Melbourne.

When questioned on what they missed most about their

lives in Italy before moving to Australia, most cited the much closer family and social relationships they had left behind in Italy. These relationships were often mentioned as being something that they missed deeply. This aspect of life in Italy certainly registered even to me when observing and trying to make comparisons between life and living there, in comparison with my own experience while living in Australia, the US and the UK.

Young Italian visitors with whom the subject of lifestyle comparisons had earlier been discussed shortly following their arrival to work in Melbourne, having later had the opportunity to experience the Australian lifestyle for a year or so, tended to offer somewhat different views. Those with whom I was able to discuss their views on life in Australia, now they had lived there for some time, expressed a preference for what they described as the more 'open' and 'much more relaxed' and 'easy-going' style of life they had been able to experience while living in Melbourne.

It seems that once they had adjusted to the environment in Melbourne, they were now finding life in Australia presented as a more attractive long-term proposition, though they understandably missed family connections back in Italy. Most also expressed the desire to settle down in Australia, in preference to returning permanently to live in Italy!

There could, of course, be a number of other reasons being responsible for such a change in attitudes.

The views expressed by younger Italian arrivals regarding their new country, brings back memories of a song made famous by Andrew Bird just after the ending of the First World War in 1918. His song "How ya gonna keep 'em down on the farm after they've seen Paree," although written in totally different circumstances to those of today, does seem to reflect a similar state-of-mind, at least as stated by young Italians living far away from the close family ties they had known back in Italy, now experiencing a different and perhaps more 'open' and 'easy-going' lifestyle in Melbourne (as they expressed it).

Family inter-relationships still seem to remain strong among many of Australia's immigrant Italian families, the grandparents of which arrived in Australia before and following the end of the Second World War. It is usually within those families and among other ethnic groups with similar backgrounds, where social changes appear to be occurring more slowly than across the rest of the population. It is also interesting to note that many young adults from Italian families, born or having grown up in Australia are tending to move away from the family home when financially able to do so.

Feeling the need

Apart from the apparent central focus of the traditional Italian family unit, it is the Italian language and how it is used that defines and projects an Italian's relationship with and feelings for their native country, its history and its unique culture.

It is also interesting to try to understand some of the differences that exist between the various languages across the world. How those differences have become reflected in some of the perhaps false perceptions we may have, when it comes to our attitude to people from significantly different cultures to our own.

Some English people for example have been known to regard their language, English, its status these days being that of the indisputable international *lingua franca*, as being a more precise language than Italian and similar others, particularly those that evolved from ancient Latin.

Maybe that idea came about and is more to do with what some around the world perceive as being the perhaps more insular, cooler, somewhat superior and reserved nature of the British, and not the source and nature of the language itself? Perhaps also the fact that internationally, English is the language used today for all international communications? That being so, some English speakers seem to have arrived at the mistaken conclusion that English is an easier to learn jungle of words and phrases than other languages?

English, contrary to that point of view, is a language where even a single letter or word can and often will be pronounced in any number of different ways, while at the same time containing individual words can have a number of different possible meanings, dependent on how and where they are being used.

English grammar may be more difficult and perhaps more inconsistent in its structure for most non-English speakers to learn or understand, than they find with Italian? Just ask any Russian Frenchman or German.

Fashion, history and opinions relating to the various language forms aside, the fact remains that a growing number of foreign visitors are finding the desire, or perhaps more accurately the need to travel to and experience Italy, overpowering.

Once there, many have also found that to learn more of that expressive, melodic, and sometimes frustrating language to get one's English-speaking tongue around, can become an all- consuming ambition.

During my first visits to Italy as part of my job working within the Australian fashion industry during the 1970s, I recall even then feeling the need to know more about the country. I also felt, for the first time, a need to become better able to understand the language. I recall that I liked the country, was intrigued by the people and places I had been able to visit so much that extending the experience into being capable of speaking at least some Italian seemed a worthwhile project.

The thinking here was that by learning more than just a few basic phrases of Italian should enable me at least to become capable of doing some sharp bartering while shopping. I was also thinking about the advantages of being able to buy a train or bus ticket, booking myself into a hotel, or arranging to hire a car.

How good it would feel just be able to excuse oneself and roll out an apology in the local vernacular in the likely event of accidentally stepping on someone's toes while wandering around in the local piazza, or during a browse around a crowded shop or supermarket.

Being capable of speaking some Italian could also assist when trying to find the direction to a church or some other historic place in which to view an ancient painting, architecture or religious relic, or something similar. To be able to ask directions would also assist when one is among the inevitable crowd of tourists, both Italian and foreign alike, and finds oneself somewhat disoriented, wandering hopefully toward or away from the *Piazza San Marco* when visiting Venice.

If you have ever tried to find the right place in Venice from which to catch a *traghetto* (ferry) to take you over to the lagoon islands of Murano, Burano or Torchello, you will also have found that the search can prove to be more than a little confusing. Such a frustrating outcome would have certainly been so having missed one or other of the directing arrows usually to be found emblazoned on the walls of a seemingly endless confusion of Venetian piazzas, stepped bridges and winding maze of seemingly endless, meandering alleyways!

There was of course another, perhaps stronger, desire on my part to be able to speak Italian, and that was to at least equip myself with enough to be able to pursue the unlikely possibility of securing a dinner date with one or other of the many attractive women I was meeting as part of my work among some of Italy's leading fashion stylists.

Feeling oneself in the grip of a deeply felt need to gain the use of its beautiful language, the question of where one needs to go, and what should one do when seeking the necessary Italian language skills? Also of some importance is the question of how long it should take to achieve a reasonable level of conversational proficiency in Italian?

Accepting what seems to be a fairly common assessment among academics and other language experts, that to become fluent in any second language will involve at least 10,000 hours of study, the pages that follow will take a somewhat different view. This particularly so when it comes to consideration of the more down-to-earth needs of a regular visitor to Italy.

If that number of hours is the minimum level of study required to enable a student to become a fully-fledged speaker of Italian, then on that basis alone there would be little hope for me, and possibly most others setting their sights on language proficiency, to reach such a goal.

I take a different view to the experts, as will already be evident. The goal I decided to set for myself was not one of becoming a fully fluent speaker of Italian. It was something lesser but practical and I believed possible to achieve, that of becoming a proficient 'communicator' in Italian, an altogether different concept – one no less of value, certainly achievable as well as being enjoyed by most wanting to travel there.

While it certainly would be a desirable outcome of my Italian studies to become fully fluent in the language, falling short of that standard should not be regarded as a failure. Nor should it represent an insurmountable limiter on the capacity of any serious adult student of Italian to enjoy the time they can spend in Italy.

For me the aim was to get myself to a point where I was in possession of sufficient Italian to enable me to communicate effectively with a native speaker. Along the way, I also gained the confidence with which to use the Italian I possessed effectively. In short, I came to recognise that what I really desired was to become capable of making my way around Italy, all the time being able to function and speak with ease, comfort and with a deep down sense of achievement.

Not fully fluent perhaps, certainly not able to draw from a fully comprehensive store of Italian vocabulary, but enough to be capable of making myself understood while travelling around Italy. The path was there to enable me to build and extend my language abilities over coming years, as I also learned more about something known as *lo stile di vita Italiano*!

5. Origins and birth of 'Standard' Italian

As a first step toward learning Italian, most people can be expected to gravitate to a local, home-based school or college offering courses in Italian. Such a step is probably the best way for anyone to commence his or her journey.

Other, luckier, people, by reason of their being born into a migrant Italian family, will of course usually find themselves in a far better position than lesser-endowed mortals.

Even then, it has often been pointed out that having had some access to the language from birth as a result of being born into or related to a family that came to Australia from a small township or village in Italy's south, Sicily, or any other locality where the locals speak mainly in a form of the language known as *dialetto* (local dialect – a language form often very different to Standard Italian) is not necessarily the total answer.

Their background may offer an advantage in one sense, but they may well find some difficulty in being able to understand the local dialect, if and when they find themselves trying to converse with people living in a similarly small village or town located in the centre or north of the country – for instance Umbria, the Veneto, Friulia-Venezia Giulia or Trentino Alto Adige etc.

Here, should they travel to such a location, they may well

find themselves unsuccessfully trying to comprehend something being said by the locals, who are not only Italians but also people who speak using the local dialect, a form very different to the style of dialect the visitor had learned from their family in Australia.

It is useful when commencing Italian studies that a student become familiar with the history of the language and how it developed. In this case understanding how what is known as Standard Italian came into being a relatively short time ago, during the country's long and often turbulent past.

Becoming appreciative of the culture from which the language derived, will go a long way toward providing a firm basis upon which to eventually develop a better feel for the language's rhythm. How the language developed is an interesting subject on its own, of value for any serious student of Italian to know a little more about.

Origins

Getting to know Italy a little better, and while trying to understand a bit more about how, what and why Italians think, feel and communicate the way they do, you will find it helpful if you were to know just a little more about the history of their language.

This aspect of your mission to learn Italian is important. It is after all the language and history that provides the form through which all cultures express their uniqueness. In this respect, Italy is no different.

Linguistically speaking, the Italian language is a member of the so-called 'Romance' group of the Italic subfamily of what is known as the 'Indo-European' family of languages.

Having now provided you with this little gem of information, you may now choose to put it to the back of your mind as it will make little if any difference to your desire to become able to speak Italian well.

But let's press on just a little further as the subject gets to be more interesting, in addition to being information that is useful for you to know.

Italian is spoken principally on the Italian peninsula, in southern Switzerland, San Marino, Sicily, Corsica, Northern Sardinia and Southern Austria as well as along the north-eastern shore of the Adriatic Sea. It is also spoken in sections of North and South America as well as across Australia, the latter more particularly since the ending of the Second World War, which saw the entry of waves of Italian immigrants arriving to settle.

Considered a single language with numerous dialects, Italian, like the other so-called Romance languages, is the direct offspring of the Latin that was originally spoken by the Romans and imposed by them on the peoples who came under their dominion.

Of all the major Romance languages, Italian retains the closest resemblance to Latin. The struggle between the written but dead language and the various forms of the living language and daily speech that is used today, most of which was derived from what has been referred to by some as 'Vulgar' Latin, was nowhere so intense or so protracted as in Italy.

How modern Italian developed

During the long period that saw the evolution of Italian, many different dialects sprang up[3]. The multiplicity of these dialects and their individual claims upon their native speakers presented a peculiar difficulty in the development of a standardised form of Italian that could reflect the cultural unity of the entire Italian peninsula.

The earliest popular Italian documents produced in the 10th century are dialectal in language, and during the following three centuries, Italian writers wrote in their native dialects, thus producing a number of competing regional schools of literature.

During the 14th century, the Tuscan dialect began to predominate, mainly because of the central and influential position of Tuscany in Italy at that time. Tuscany also became dominant because of the aggressive commerce of its then most important city, Florence. Moreover, of all the Italian dialects, Tuscan departs least in morphology and phonology from classical Latin, and it therefore harmonises best with the Italian traditions of Latin culture.

Finally, Florentine culture served to produce the three literary artists who best summarised Italian thought and feeling dur-

---

[3]The dialects of modern Italy all have their roots in the spoken form of Latin (so-called Vulgar Latin), in use throughout the Roman Empire. Vulgar Latin had its own local peculiarities even before the fall of the Empire. The political instability that followed Roman rule kept Italy from re-uniting as a nation until the 19th century. This long period of fragmentation, and the fact that Classical Latin was preferred as the international language of study, allowed the various modes of speech to develop on their own until they could almost be called separate languages. Many dialects are, in fact, unintelligible with each other.

ing the late Middle Ages and early Renaissance: Dante, Petrarca and Boccaccio.

Accademia della Crusca,[4] or the 'Academy of the Bran' as it was first known, was originally founded in Florence in 1582. Still in existence today *Accademia della Crusca* was the first such institution in Europe, and the first to produce a modern national language.

Later that century after the *Accademia* was first founded in Florence, its objective then was: "to maintain the purity of the language." The major work of the society was the compilation of A. F. Grazzini's *Vocabulario*, a dictionary of so described pure words, first published in 1612 and later taken on as a model by other European states. It was also becoming apparent by then that Standard Italian was no longer a theoretical concept but a viable linguistic entity, regardless of whether or not anyone actually spoke it.

Another watershed in the evolution of Standard Italian was the publication of *I Promessi Sposi*, an Italian historical novel written by Alessandro Manzoni, first published in 1827. Manzoni's famous quote *"lavare i panni in Arno"* in part referred to the influence of the Florentine vernacular on his work. He actually revised and republished the novel in the Tuscan idiom (Manzoni himself was from Milan) in a deliberate effort to promote a language that he hoped would be commonly used and understood by most Italians.

The novel, considered a masterpiece of world literature at

---

[4] *Academia della Crusca*, accessed 1 June 2016, http://www.accademiadellacrusca.it/

the time, is a paradigm for the modern Italian language and is still widely read and studied. Many expressions, quotes and names from the novel are still commonly used in Italian.

National and linguistic unification

Not long after *I Promessi Sposi* was published, the various states of the Italian peninsula were unified into the single state of Italy after a series of military battles, political upheaval, and social movements. One of the platforms that motivated some of the reformists was the idea of Italian as the national language.

* * *

Note

Interestingly, only an estimated 2.5% of Italy's population could speak what eventually became known as Standard Italian when it became a unified nation in 1861.

* * *

That situation gradually changed, particularly when Rome became Italy's capital. The inflow of people from all over Italy turned the city into a virtual linguistic laboratory, where Standard Italian gradually became a spoken language.

Just a few years later, Milan joined Rome in this role, mainly due to its rapid industrialisation which of itself recreated a situation in which immigrants flocked into the city and local region where they needed to be able to communicate with other people from all over Italy.

Standard Italian, anyone?

Given the complex route that Standard Italian has taken – from *la vulgata dantesca* to what one writer termed as "Corn flakes and crusty Florentines", from Manzoni's laundry (being washed in the river Arno) to being declared the national language of a new nation in which almost no one spoke it!

Who speaks Standard Italian today? Well, almost everyone … and yet at times, no one!

Today, children in every region across Italy are taught Standard Italian in school, and perhaps also the regional dialect used by their parents and grandparents at home. There is some evidence that general use of regional dialects appears to be gradually declining as years pass and new generations evolve.

Some purists regard such a trend as being detrimental to the language, particularly as some of the more Americanised styles of speaking and writing are becoming incorporated into everyday Italian. This trend is occurring mainly as a result of the growing popularity of American/English language music, movies, TV programmes, internationally branded products and services, newspapers and news broadcasts.

Recent years have also seen more and more English style words and terminology being incorporated into everyday Italian usage.

Most Italians, when speaking, often use variations in the language along a continuum from Standard Italian to regional and local dialects, according to what is appropriate to their part of the country. Their speech patterns also have variations and tend toward an intonation that is typical of that part of the country from which they originated.

Comment

It can reasonably be said today that nearly every Italian, at least most of those under the age of a hundred years, should be capable of understanding, if not generally using Standard Italian.

* * *

I found a good illustration of one problem with non-standard Italian (*dialetto*) during a visit to southern Italy. This was my first visit to the country during the 1970s, the visit to which I referred earlier.

At the time I was capable of remembering a few words picked up in the north, one or two verbs and at least a couple of phrases in Standard Italian, in addition to *si, per favore, grazie*. What I was actually confronted with, though, on entering an *osteria* (hotel/inn) in the small town in which I had planned to stay for the night – my blundering attempts to reply to or even begin to understand a simple question from the local owner of the establishment proving futile – was something else. The scene might well at the time have appeared similar to that of a comedic John Cleese–inspired Monty Python sketch!

In addition to the owner, other customers, most who appeared to be locals, were speaking a form of the language that seemed far removed from the kind of Italian I had been hearing in Milan. To make things worse, everyone spoke with the speed of a springtime mountain stream in flood. Words virtually bubbled along and phrases tumbled into one another in great confusion, regardless of my attempted plea, at one time, for them to speak a little slower.

Of course the people there, like most I met then and others I have met since over the length and breadth of Italy during years of visiting, were kind and understanding toward me, then a relatively ignorant foreigner.

I was rapidly becoming desperate, unable to stretch my Italian much beyond a nod of the head (indicating that I understood what they were trying to convey to me – which in almost all cases I didn't), or indicating various parts of my body, for instance my mouth as an indication of my need to drink or eat, or my need to use the toilet. Even trying to order my dinner proved a near impossibility. This was eventually achieved by me pointing to what it was that I thought I might like to order from the unpronounceable menu that offered such strange sounding dishes as *Antipasti, Primi Piatti, Secondi, Contorni, Insalata, Dolci* etc., all being offered as part of *cena* (dinner).

Thankfully, I eventually found myself tucking into a deliciously cooked dinner, in spite of not understanding more than a word or two of the menu or much of my host's attempts at an explanation. My meal that evening, together with a sample glass, or two, or even three of the local brand of what looked to be home brewed *vino rosso* (red wine), left me with at least some good feelings of contentment as the evening rolled on.

I tumbled into bed that night in a small town in the south, a pretty place with an almost unpronounceable name. I was feeling more than a little dizzy from the wine, but at least I had a full stomach. I was also feeling a great deal more in the form of acute frustration at not being able to communicate with my hosts and fellow diners. When added to the frustrations of not being able to hold a conversation with the girl and her friends that I had met just a few days earlier in the Milan discotheque, the experience was now also leaving me feeling a little depressed and somewhat disoriented.

While the food the previous evening had been tasty, I found

myself having to dine more or less in silence for most of the time, until a fellow diner with some English came over to ask how I liked being in Italy.

At dawn the next day, I awoke with the makings of a massive headache alongside a sizeable hangover from the wine.

Once my head had cleared and I was able to think more clearly, I firmly decided, there and then, that whatever the cost, inconvenience or difficulty involved with learning at least sufficient Italian to enable me to communicate better on my next visit, I would seek to enrol myself in an Italian school on my return to Melbourne.

6. *Where to from here?*

Progress toward the achievement of at least some competency in Italian is possible even if a student is limited, both by their distance from the country whose language they desire to master, or them having a limited amount of spare time and/or funds at their disposal.

To extend this point a little further, it is my view that any person having the desire and motivation to succeed in their quest to become a proficient speaker of Italian, but not in possession of a great deal of spare time – or the ability to spend a long period in Italy – can still achieve a reasonable level of language proficiency. They can obtain the capacity to speak Italian, though they will always recognise some limitations, particularly when it comes to the question of the level they are capable of achieving.

Most things are possible, always providing a student is really intent and fully motivated toward becoming a proficient speaker, and are prepared to commit themselves to a regular programme of disciplined self-study that includes a few learning aids and practical exercises.

This sounds simple enough, but carrying out such a programme at the level of concentration required may well prove to be less effort than some may be prepared to bring to the task.

'Multifaceted' learning is another descriptor I have chosen to use here. It refers to the careful selection and regular use of a select, not necessarily wide, range of learning aids and exercises, each being included on the basis of their capacity to enhance and assist the process of language learning and retention. In other words, areas of study comprising learning aids selected because they are able to help the student improve their capacity to learn, absorb, fix and later use the vocabulary and related knowledge gained – with confidence.

For some students, their study of Italian will be limited, serving mainly to represent an interesting pastime. An absorbing but not a too serious attempt to complete what they may originally have thought to achieve. A thought bubble perhaps, one that had originally come to mind during a visit to Italy, something that they had not been prepared to follow up with the level of commitment such a task requires.

All they really desire is to retain just enough of the language to get themselves to a point where they can move around the country with at least some comfort when called upon to speak.

The kind of student I have in mind here most probably seeks to become capable of retaining a little Italian, with perhaps a few relatively easy to learn phrases. Happy that is, but without anything in the way of a consuming desire to eventually become capable of involving themselves in a higher level of conversation, one requiring a much broader range of vocabulary, together with the confidence to use it.

If they are seriously intent on going much further toward becoming a proficient Italian speaker, it is a primary necessity that the student thinks carefully as to the level of effort they are prepared to commit to before embarking upon any course of language training.

Starting out

The most productive way for any student to commence their journey is for them to locate and enrol in a well-credentialed local Italian language school. Usually this will be in the form of an established Italian community sponsored language centre, one ideally located close by in their city, town or local suburb.

Before making a final commitment to any such courses, it is important to ensure that those staffing the course are native Italian speakers, fully qualified to teach the language.

You may be surprised to learn that some advertising themselves as fully qualified course providers are not necessarily qualified to teach. They may well be reasonably or even very fluent in Italian, but when it comes to their ability to teach, they lack the necessary skills, formal qualifications and, most importantly, an 'innovative imagination'.

My first, and probably also your, initial venture into familiarity with the Italian language, came in the form of enrolling myself into a course run by the local Italian community. In my case, this was Melbourne's Centre of Italian Studies.

This organisation, known locally as CIS, is based in the inner northern Melbourne suburb of Carlton. Information on this school is included in the References section).

The CIS course proved to be a good starting point. It provided most of the basic grammar and a reasonably broad range of vocabulary, which was what I then needed to get me going. As I progressed through toward the later stages of the course, I eventually found myself at a point at which it was becoming clear that learning to speak well in Italian was going to need much more than a further few months more of what had developed into a relatively static form of language education. In short, I was beginning to find that the style of tuition I had been undergoing to date, being mainly book based with one or two other support aids, together with teaching sessions I was only able to attend on a once-weekly basis, was not going to meet my needs.

Italian grammar is so different

As the initial weeks of the course progressed, it was also becoming clear that Italian grammar was more than just a little different to that of English.

With Italian grammar having its basis in Latin and English having developed over the centuries from dialects and languages originating from a wider variety of sources, including Latin, this was my first lesson in the realities that came with being an adult native English speaker trying to master a Latin-based second language.

An example of one important difference with English, other than the Latinate grammar format of Italian, was that Italians had totally different forms of words and phrases to describe objects, people and places as being either masculine or feminine. This, of course, necessitated the learning and correct application of the different word forms used to describe those differences. While that complicated things a little at first, the situation got even *more* complicated, as there didn't appear to be any clear rules applying to this aspect of the language. At least, there seemed no rules that I could understand. For instance, why had an object or place been deemed either masculine or feminine in the first place?

Some descriptions of gender were obvious, such as when it came to the differences between a man (*un uomo*) and a woman (*una donna*), a boy (*un ragazzo*) or girl (*una ragazza*), he (*lui*) and she (*lei*). Others, though, like why a table (*il tavolo*) is spoken of as being masculine while the chair that one sits on at the table is regarded as being feminine (*la sedia*) being more difficult to fathom. More was to come on the question of gender, some even more difficult to understand. Things were beginning to get progressively cloudier the further my studies progressed.

Getting used to the masculinity and femininity of objects spoken of in Italian was but one aspect that added to the complexity of the language, but then I also learned that Italians had a different set of verbs that referred to situations and issues which had occurred in the more remote past. Individual verbs that were different to those used to describe events that had occurred in the recent past. Somewhat different, of course from the way modern English is used.

While this was a little confusing, here again there appeared to be no rule by which to define exactly when use of the remote past form of a verb became necessary. Was it to be used 10+, 50+, 100+ or 1,000+ years in the past?

And, there was even more to contend with as I also learned that with Italian there are different forms of speech expected should the speaker be addressing a stranger as opposed to a family member, close friend or just a work colleague! Etiquette also entered into the scene in Italian when it came to the use of different forms of salutation, either formal or informal. I also learned that there were various forms to be used should you find yourself greeting, speaking or answering a close relative, friend, stranger or superior.

These modes of address of course added yet another dimension to the task. In modern English, such language forms rarely apply, particularly in relatively relaxed Australia, except perhaps to be expected when addressing royalty, prime ministers and High Court judges – not a very regular day-to-day situation, thank goodness.

Following a few initial months of study, not only did I find myself having to learn how to conjugate lots of different 'regular' and 'irregular' verbs, some exceedingly long and difficult to even get my English-speaking tongue around, but I also found it difficult to get to grips with the correct combination, order and pronunciation of Italian words, to describe or discuss something or other that I wished to communicate. Add to that of course having to decide whether the object, place or whatever else one wished to describe was either of the masculine or feminine variety, or someone considered being either superior or inferior – at least to my perceived status in life!

Italian was by now getting to be quite complicated, certainly for this relatively laid back and usually informal speaker of English!

Beyond that, and on the plus side, I was to some extent lucky in my Italian studies at the time, in that the then lady in my life was a Melbourne-born lass of Italian extraction, the daughter of *dialetto*-speaking Italian parents. Both her parents and the greater part of their families had migrated to Australia during the years following the Second World War. Nearly all hailed from or around the small township of Conco, located north among the hill country between Marostica and more northerly Asiago, in the Veneto province.

She did assist me to gradually extend my then-basic vocabulary to a few more adventurous words and phrases. Not much more, though, as later my then companion, possessing very little in the way of patience when trying to deal with my admittedly stumbling attempts and need for assistance with written exercises in Standard Italian grammar, finally gave up on me and proffered the advice: "keep going to the local Italian classes being offered by CIS!"

This was good advice, but I then found that without sufficient practice and the use of additional learning aids, there was little possibility of using and developing my Italian beyond what I was learning at my weekly Italian classes..

I also began to suspect that even to my then companion, the finer points of written Italian grammar were somewhat outside her capacity to assist me with. This was probably more to do with the fact that the Italian side of her bilingual abilities had come about as a result of her inheritance of the spoken dialect of her parents, coming as they did from a small, mainly dialect-speaking township located in the very picturesque northern Italian *altipiani* (high plains).

She spoke fluent Italian in the idiom of that part of the country from which her family had migrated. Even then, her Italian, like so many other first-generation Australians born of Italian parents, was interspersed regularly with a fair sprinkling of what I think best described as 'Aussie/English' words, and was thus of little use to me at the level I was then at in my studies.

I did continue to read as much as I could, and got by with the purchase of a couple of Italian illustrated children's reading books. They helped a little when it came to picking up a bit more in the way of vocabulary, but of course even that fell a short of enabling me to advance much further in my quest to be able to share in even a basic level of Italian conversation.

I even tried, at times, to read a copy of the local *Il Globo* newspaper, bought from a local Italian milk bar. That also failed to assist me a great deal as the style of writing, the vocabulary used and combination of words left me struggling to make any sense out of what was written, even with the assistance of my trusty Italian/English dictionary.

Frustration was beginning to set in at this stage, mainly due to my inability to make a great deal of sense out of written Italian.

I should of course have realised that what I was trying to do had outstripped my capabilities at that relatively early stage of my studies, particularly when it came to trying to read an Italian language newspaper.

By that time, I had also come to the not too happy conclusion that I would need to regroup and reset my thinking more along the lines of doing much more for myself on a more regular basis, but outside attendance at what had become a relatively stalled method of learning.

The CIS programme had provided me with a solid foundation from which to develop, but it had also become apparent that there were other issues involved, particularly when it came to becoming more capable of absorbing more of the language I needed. Some of my thinking then began to revolve around the possibility of finding and eventually using other kinds of aids to learning, plus the need for a great deal more dedicated practice and regular revision if I was to progress much further. I had arrived at the first barrier to my progress.

As to the CIS course, it should be noted that even though it is one of the best to be found in Australia for any beginner or later learner to use as part of their journey, those running the CIS programme make the questionable claim on their website that "Our courses are very practical, conversational courses which will have you speaking in Italian from day 1".

Such a claim is misleading, as well as being a not very helpful starting point for any student about to commence their Italian studies.

At the time, even I was capable of remembering a number of simple words in Italian after just a few hours' tuition. A word or two or even a short phrase was also possible following a couple of weeks tuition, but certainly not anywhere near the level that I would regard as being able to "speak Italian from day 1".

Being capable of speaking Italian, to me at least, should mean much more than a few short phrases. Any statement referring to a student becoming able to speak Italian should be used more in terms of them being capable of conducting a relatively simple but understandable conversation. This is also linked to being able to read and correctly pronounce written Italian text from a book using a relatively simple form of Standard Italian grammar, for example a book written specifically for children (certainly not including literature similar in nature to the *Divina Commedia*, Dante Alighieri's Italian masterpiece!).

I'm not sure why an organisation like CIS feels the need to advertise their language-teaching services using what amounts to such a questionable promise. I know that from my own perspective, even while I was a student at CIS's Carlton based language school, I (and others in my classes at the time) found it more than a little disappointing not to have been able to progress faster, beyond the relatively low level of understanding I had been able to gain even by the later stages of their course.

Perhaps, at the time, I had expected too much, after reading CIS's unnecessary promise to have me speaking Italian from day one. Of course, the speaking of Italian at the level I was aiming for at the time was totally unrealistic.

The size of classes could also have had something to do with any limitations when it came to the level of progress I was able to achieve at that time. The larger the group of students being tutored, the more difficult it was during each teaching session for any one tutor to spend much time with each individual student.

It had been many long years since I had studied English grammar at school … and from memory, I even had difficulties with that at the time. So, was there any hope for me with Italian?

7. After language school ... what then?

Following my progression through the various stages of tuition at CIS it was fast becoming clear that to progress further toward my goal of becoming a reasonably proficient speaker of Italian, I needed to look beyond CIS to other learning options.

I was beginning to find, as my studies progressed, that while it may well be interesting from an academic standpoint to continue trying to gain proficiency in my chosen second language via a classroom style environment, the means by which to progress to a more effective learning process would need to involve studies and practice different in scope. Different, at least, from what I had to work with to date.

What form that different learning format should be was unclear. I did however have an as yet undefined sense that if I were to progress much further, I would need to change to something other than the kind of learning process to which I had tied myself so far.

How could I achieve this other than by living in Italy? At that at time, it was out of the question. I did, however, have a sense that continuing to attend classes at CIS, or even some other similarly organised formal classroom situation in Australia, was not the answer. Not the answer, at least, for me. The question now had become one of what to do next.

In the short term, my problem was partially resolved as a result of a previously planned business visit that was to take me to Europe a year or so following commencement of my studies in Melbourne.

Following that business visit while still in Europe, I decided to call a time out and enrol myself in a month-long Italian residential course.

The decision to join this particular course in Italy was in the hope that with some months of Italian studies thus far under my belt, a month of training in Italy could well enable me to get around or over the wall that I now found barring my progress. I was hoping that a month or so of solid study and practice in Italy would enable me to improve my capacity to conduct at least a relatively simple form of conversation.

The ideal place it seemed at the time would be to enrol at the Italian *Universita per Stranieri* (University for Foreigners), a venerable Perugia-based institution, well known internationally.

Perugia is a very interesting city, dating back to the early Etruscan era. The university, a single free-standing building located just outside Perugia's remaining city gate, forms an impressive entry to the historical centre of the city, much as the nearby Etruscan-era stone gate had done for over a millennium.

Had I not at the time been able to travel beyond Australia on business, I might have contemplated enrolling myself in one or other of the self-styled 'advanced' courses in Italian being offered by one or other of the various private tutors, colleges and universities. As things stood at the time though, together with the fact that I would be travelling to Europe on business that year, why not enrol myself in a world-renowned university in Italy?

The *Universita per Stranieri*[5] is said to be one of the oldest established Italian language-teaching institutions. The course of interest to me at the time, a summer school, was dedicated specifically to teaching the Italian language to foreign students. It seemed then that this just might be the place of learning to meet my currently felt needs. To continue my further studies in Perugia was beginning to feel as though I was now well on my way...

Universita per Stranieri, Perugia Italy

On enrolment day in Perugia, I joined a small group of other adult Australian students and thus found myself eagerly looking forward to making the hoped for progress with conversational Italian.

I was about to join what eventually turned out to be a large group of students. The group that assembled in Perugia seemed an enthusiastic crowd. At registration, most of us were excitedly expressing our joy just being there and in Italy. Everyone was hopeful – drawn to that historic city like moths to a light globe.

The student intake at that venerable centre of language learning had been drawn from the four corners of the known world. There were Russians, Ukrainians, Japanese, Americans, British, Germans, a couple of others of unknown or undefined heritage, one or two students of Eastern European extraction, just to name a few – and a group of eight Australians.

---

[5](See References section for details).

Following our arrival in Perugia, every student was required to complete a preliminary written examination. This was designed to determine the level of Italian claimed by each student. All then were subsequently allocated to different class levels, according to how the two-page test had been answered.

Most of the questions posed left me more than a little perplexed, as I for one must admit that I had to date achieved only a basic level of understanding and retention of Italian grammar. What else I could honestly claim to know at the time was being capable of conjugating some of the better-known Italian verbs and the sometimes-correct use of a narrow range of personal and other pronouns.

Most of the more important written stuff, however, had me and I suspect more than a few other of my colleagues struggling.

Following registration and the results of the language test having been analysed by the teaching staff, what had developed into a large crowd of students was divided into different groups, each group being allocated to a tutor. Significantly, most of us Australians and what appeared to be a large proportion of the other new students had been allocated into what we were then given to understand as being a lower-level grouping, something designated as being in the order of 'basic to intermediate'.

Apart from instructions and everything else being entirely in Italian, which to most of us foreign students understandably proved to be difficult to follow, the size of our group, much larger than anything I had encountered back in Melbourne, left me with the distinct feeling that the teaching arrangements being made by the university would leave little opportunity to expect much more than a relatively shallow approach to the tuition.

It also became obvious, from the size of my group, that there would be less opportunity to deal with subjects and issues on a more personal basis. This, unfortunately, turned out to be the case.

English, Russian, German and the other native tongues of my colleagues were not allowed. This was understandable, of course, as we were there to learn Italian. Thus we previously unsuspecting month-long students were forced to concentrate more on the job in hand, in both written and spoken Italian.

It seemed that few teaching staff would be made available to break my group down into manageable smaller groups of students. This proved to be a major drawback with the course.

Two weeks into the course, in spite of the size of my group, some Italian at last began to seep into my brain and I was at last becoming better able to understand some of what our patient tutor was endeavouring to explain.

There was lots of written homework, along with texts for us to study and learn. This did assist the process a little, but the size of our group and our single tutor's capacity to deal effectively with the variety of nationalities present, made the time allowed for the asking and answering of questions very short. Another limitation was that questions requesting clarification on one or other point of grammar were sometimes unable to be discussed and clarified in sufficient detail, explanations sometimes proving difficult to understand, always having to be delivered in Italian!

I am not aware of how the university's courses were conducted at other times of the year, but in the case of the summer course I attended, with the number of students involved there should at least have been more tutors and smaller group sizes provided.

The obvious difficulties involved trying to teach Italian to a group of adult foreign students, all arriving from different countries and with some even possessing less Italian than I, the task for any tutor would have been difficult.

Areas of grammar and vocabulary that really needed to be covered in greater depth proved difficult to cover, reducing the potential effectiveness of the course. Practice with conversation was barely touched if at all, other than in the form of short question-and-answer periods during each session.

I eventually emerged, not yet anywhere near conversationally adequate following my month in Perugia, at least having received a better sense of the structure of Italian grammar. I had been able to gather some extra verbs, learned how to conjugate them and recite a few phrases that I practiced extensively in front of the mirror in my rented accommodation, housed as I was under the eaves of one of the rows of terraced houses located in the old part of the city.

I was also introduced to the Italian singer Eros Ramazzotti and his popular songs of the day, a selection of which was being used in what the university referred to as its Language Laboratory. Use even of the laboratory as part of the strategy to get our ears tuned in more to being able to listen to spoken and sung Italian was also a little scanty. I did however manage to learn some of the words of one or two of Eros's songs, but not much more.

And what of the accommodation in Perugia? That of course was quite old and provided what could be described as an interestingly ancient Italian experience.

You could tell the accommodation was more ancient than just old, apart from the crumbling external structure of the building, creaky and uncarpeted staircase and difficult to open windows and no air-conditioning.

The toilet facilities along with the building were definitely medieval. These came in the form of a sinister-looking black hole strategically located in the centre of the floor of my tiny bathroom, over which one was required to stand or squat when carrying out one or other of the regularly necessary functions of the human digestive and lower intestinal systems. Thus I was for the first time introduced to an Italian 'hole-in-the-floor' style toilet facility.

This, for some, could be most uncomfortable, and there wasn't even a bidet to be seen! The shower plumbing, in concert with the apartment's surroundings, was incapable of keeping the flow of lukewarm water above the absolute minimum, particularly if more than one other person in the building was using the plumbing system at the same time. All this made it extremely difficult to get even a shallow lather up when trying to wash one's body and hair. It became a case of rising as early as possible to beat the rush, particularly when it came to showering.

But then, we were, after all, resident in what remained of an ancient, very interesting to explore Etruscan city. It was to be expected that all the above restrictions would apply in some way or other, the accommodation serving as it did to add further to the experience of living for a short time in an ancient Etruscan city.

My apartment accommodation, which should more accurately be described as an attic, had an opening skylight set in the roof above my bed. When I could summon up enough strength to lift it up and place the also ancient-looking wooden pole under its rim, enabled a fabulous view across the city and well beyond.

On the social side of things, the weeks spent in and around

Perugia proved to be the real highlight of my time there. Most evenings were spent getting together with colleagues from a few of the other groups of students, either at a cook-up in one or other of the student apartments or rooms, or a session in the university's cafeteria or local bar somewhere outside the historical part of the city.

While at times getting together with other international students and trying to develop a conversation in Italian, this usually reverted, even on the part of most of the non-English-speaking students, to the use of English, as we all soon exhausted our capacity to get much beyond a scrappy sentence or two of conversational Italian. Most of our attempts at maintaining a conversation in Italian, generally delivered in doubtful, often 'scratchy' Italian proved short-lived. This served to confirm that English really is the world's *lingua franca*, 'the language used for convenience between different people(s)'.

It was also interesting to find that most of the non-English students possessed at least some conversational English, so from that standpoint communication with them was found to be relatively easy, much easier than trying to converse in our limited Italian! I also suspect that more than a few of our non-English-speaking colleagues were welcoming the opportunity thus presented to be able to use and improve their English.

All in all, the live-in course in Perugia proved to be an interesting and different kind of month away from home, spent gaining more Italian and meeting new people – all in an ancient Etruscan city. It couldn't get much better than that, at least when it came to the location and new people I was able to meet during the course. Visits to various historic and other interesting locations around Perugia like Assisi, Sienna, Orvieto, Montepulciano and other local townships, served also to extend my knowledge of the surrounding countryside.

Shopping for food when cooking for myself in my small under the eaves apartment usually took place at the local supermarket or nearby farmer's market, all of which assisted in a slow but gradual improvement in my understanding and day-to-day usage of simple Italian. The produce was mainly sourced from local farms, fresh and relatively well priced, too, in comparison to similar in Australia.

Did my month-long stay in Perugia assist in my quest? Yes, partly, but I later found that there were other, more personalised styles of language course also on offer in Italy, which for most foreign students would have proved better able to provide a more positive way of improving their conversational Italian. Many of these courses, I subsequently learned, were designed and organised in a manner aimed at providing a more conducive study environment among a smaller, more manageable group of students.

The University of Perugia staff tended to teach the subject in very much the same way as any academic institution would be expected to, the tutor/lecturer speaking to a relatively large group of students, concentrating mainly on the more technical aspects of the language.

Most of the students I got to speak with were more intent on gaining the capacity to speak better Italian, as opposed to just gaining a more academically oriented handle on the language.

What most of us had been hoping for were smaller student groups and more concentration on the conversational side of the subject. In retrospect, this was not what the university, in this instance at least, seemed capable or perhaps interested in providing.

This is not to say that the month of study spent in Italy

was wasted. Any attendance at a well-organised tertiary level learning institution would be worth the effort. That is, provided the intending part-time student is at an advanced enough stage of their studies at which to find the style of teaching of some benefit.

On returning to Australia and now having to catch up on business commitments, I eventually lost much of what I had gained in Perugia. That of course was not the fault of the university. Much of what I had gained, apart from some of the personal contacts made while there, had faded nearly as quickly as they had been learned. This further emphasised the importance of working on a regular basis, possibly with a different kind of learning regime, to retain as much as possible of the language being learned. Of course, living many thousands of kilometres from Italy only served to make the task more difficult.

Lessons learned here did not go unnoticed.

More language school

My next foray into Italian studies, once I had time to settle back down to some sort of regular routine in Melbourne, came in the form of what was advertised as being a more advanced local course (more advanced than CIS, they claimed). This was a privately owned and run language school based in Melbourne's southern suburbs. This course used a series of tapes, in addition to their preferred text and grammar publications, a combination of which together with a course tutor were supposed to be sufficient to enable a student to become capable of reading Italian, while concurrently gaining the use of a greater range of Italian vocabularies.

This and other locally based courses I tried, while interesting and useful when it came to reading and receiving a little more in the way of practice with what amounted mainly to question-and-answer conversations, in and of themselves were unable, particularly within the time available at the school, to offer much more toward assisting my capacity to listen, absorb, retain and ultimately to gain the confidence to actually use even the range of Italian vocabulary I then held. While my reading of Italian texts did improve, as did my capacity to complete most of the written phrases required amid a great deal of written homework between classes, my as yet inability to use whatever Italian vocabulary I had been able to gather to date was a different matter.

It was about this time that the need to find another way of developing my capacity to listen and absorb the language became clearer. I felt the need to at least try to recreate a more interesting and creative learning environment to enter as part of any ongoing language studies. This learning routine had to at least go some way toward the simulation of something approaching an Italian environment (an understandably difficult task) and, if possible, to create a format within which I could also begin to learn and absorb some of the more intricate and subtle characteristics and rhythms of spoken Italian.

Other learning options

Some individual language tutors do offer the opportunity of a series of one-on-one style learning sessions. This approach usually involves a tutor with a single student. They may also include up to two, perhaps three others.

Provided you can find a fully qualified tutor, and are also capable of affording the expected higher cost involved with more than just a single one-on-one session per week – such an arrangement could make a vast difference. Unfortunately, I had neither the time nor the funds to spare at the time to proceed along that path.

While on the subject of one-on-one tutoring, there are a number of such service offerings, usually being provided by individual, private tutors.

One such service available in Melbourne uses the title "*Mani in Pasta*" (Have a finger in the pie). This is an Italian language service offered by a qualified Italian tutor that I was able to discuss during research for this book. There will of course be other locally based tutors of a similar nature to be found in most capital cities. Before making a commitment to any one of these services, however, it would be useful to try to get some idea of the teaching expertise of the person offering them.

The *Mani in Pasta* concept interestingly also offered the option, if required by the student, of a format that linked the practical use of conversational Italian with the preparation of some simple Italian dishes. Another programme is designed specifically to interest and tutor young children.

Mani in Pasta and the concept, upon which this one-on-one teaching course was developed, is described in the References section. Other local tutors also offer similar kinds of services.

This form of tutoring by its very nature seeks to provide an opportunity to improve a student's understanding and practical use of everyday Italian. The student involved can gain practice with the actual use of idiomatic Italian throughout each tutoring session. Having to converse solely in Italian will provide a student with an opportunity to develop more confidence, particularly when it comes to them gaining the capacity to think more easily in an Italian mode.

The cost of one-on-one tutoring, if it is intended that it be used on a regular basis, is something in need of careful consideration.

On the question of having sufficient study time available, I would suspect that there are students of Italian who from time to time have found it necessary to delay or take a break from their studies due to personal, family or business demands.

My need to take a break from my Italian studies around that period was also due to family pressures. Also, at the time, the demands of my business activities had increased to the point where I was no longer able to maintain a regular programme of necessary studies. Both issues, coming as they did at the same time, conspired to push my Italian studies a little way down my priority list.

While I still tried to retain as much as possible of what Italian I had gained to date, my business activities, travel demands and other issues made my attempts to regularly allocate time for study almost impossible. A consequence of this meant that I began to lose much of what had been absorbed to that time

8. Isn't there a quicker way?

Good question this – to which there are a couple of equally good answers, neither providing a satisfactory solution, particularly so in the case of any intending student finding that they are limited to an irregular pattern of spare time in which to study and practice.

The fact is that there is no really 'sure-fire' quick way by which to learn Italian, to learn it sufficiently well enough to become capable of speaking and conducting a conversation with confidence! Experience has also shown that where opportunities to study and practice according to a regular timetable became sparse or become non-existent for even a relatively short period, the lack of continuity resulted in the loss of much of what I had earlier absorbed. This factor alone points to the need always to continue working on a regular basis. Living so far from Italy and day-to-day access to spoken Italian, also highlighted the importance of maintaining a regular routine of study and practice, always with at least some form of vocal learning aid being included.

While there may be no quick solution to becoming fully fluent in the language, I was eventually able to improve my capacity to learn, absorb and even found myself able to retain more of what I was learning and practicing. This became possible only later, when I at last was able to commit myself to a regular routine of study and practice.

Success came eventually, but not before I was able to accommodate myself to a regular regime of personal study, practice and constant repetition. While this formed an important part of the process, the judicious use of a small, select group of learning aids, together with some additional exercises also played an important part in my programme.

Part-time adult learning of Italian will inevitably prove be a relatively slow process. The process will be slower than one would expect with a young child, but understandable considering the number of (native) monolingual years most adult students have thus far experienced. Difficulties with pronunciation will also feel strange, particularly during the earlier stages during which the student needs to gain a good working understanding of Italian grammar, while at the same time trying to cope with learning how to pronounce a new and often 'strange' form of words.

The speed at which any individual should then expect to advance will depend to a large extent on his or her attitude when it comes to the level of discipline they are prepared to apply to their personal study programme. This will eventually need to include some form of self-imposed study – practical work undertaken outside or in addition to any classroom-based courses they may also be planning to attend.

Some may prefer to continue solely on the basis of a classroom-based programme of study, perhaps in the fond hope of eventually achieving something close to fluency in Italian. But I have found that there is much more to be gained, once having reached what is generally regarded as being at or just beyond 'intermediate' level studies, by then moving on to a well-considered programme of self-study.

The kind of aids and support activities I will be defining

later do not include initially trying to understand everything that is being said during a broadcast of Italian TV news and radio broadcasts being beamed through a local station. While these programmes are being rebroadcast on the SBS network and are accessible on the Internet throughout Australia, most students will find Italian sourced broadcasts beamed later via SBS difficult to follow. A similar situation will also apply in other English-speaking countries.

Trying to understand spoken Italian as it is presented on Italian sourced TV or radio broadcasts depends on the watcher or listeners' level of comprehension, their capacity to absorb and react to a broad enough range of vocabulary, accessible at the speed by which it is being spoken by the TV or radio presenter. A considerable task! Comprehension also depends to a large extent on the clarity and speed with which the Italian commentator or newsreader is speaking – often very quickly and usually too quick for any early stage student to keep up with! The addition of visuals in support of what an Italian TV newsreader is reporting will offer some assistance even to a beginner, but not much more.

Do not expect to get anywhere in advance of that status, at least until you are much further advanced in your capacity to absorb and understand the cadence and flow of the language being presented by a native Italian speaker. This is and will continue to be a difficult task, unless of course you just happen to meet up with a TV or radio presenter who speaks with clear diction, uses simple phrases and speaks slowly. I have heard only one such broadcaster thus far, and he was in Australia and speaking on the *Rete Italia* network.

The news here

Do not be dismayed if you cannot fathom much of what is being reported on Italian TV or radio and maybe only a little of what you find written in one or other of Italy's national and local newspapers.

Becoming capable of getting yourself up to a full level of comprehension when listening to the radio, reading a newspaper or watching TV will only come once having obtained a firm grasp of conversational Italian. That will take a great deal longer than becoming capable of conducting a simple conversation in Italian. Even then, like newspapers the world over, words, phraseology, descriptions and headlines as used by Italian newspapers, are often presented in the form of something sometimes referred to as 'newspaper-speak'. In other words, language not necessarily following precisely the form of Standard Italian.

By this time, you should be in no doubt that there is no such thing as a shortcut to gaining sufficient Italian to enable you to listen efficiently and with complete understanding.

It should also have become clear by now that there is a need always to push yourself beyond the inevitable barriers that will confront you as you continue toward your goal. This is one of the key issues to eventually becoming able to remove yourself temporarily from your native English. Even then, progress only becomes possible following diligent practice and constant daily work.

Even if following a daily study routine you, like me, will also need to accept the fact that you will not always be capable of remembering the correct form of the Italian words and phrases that will be needed during a conversation. Correct, that is, in the form that a native Italian speaker would use them. What is more important here though is becoming able to demonstrate to whichever Italian you are trying to hold a conversation with, that you are at least trying hard to do some justice to their beautiful language!

Italians, unlike the French and I fear many English speakers, always seem willing to forgive most of the inevitable mistakes being made by a foreign visitor. Usually mistakes will be forgiven and, more importantly, you will more often than not find yourself being encouraged and complimented for your efforts.

Stuttering attempts to speak Italian will usually be rewarded with at least some form of a compliment from whomever you are speaking with at the time, possibly along the lines of *Veramente lei parle bene l'Italiano!* (truly, you speak Italian well!).

When and if you eventually get to visit Italy and begin to meet up with native Italians, stress always that you want to speak only in Italian. Even though you will inevitably make mistakes along the way with pronouns, personal and otherwise, incorrect conjugation of verbs, words or phrases etc., you will usually be understood. You will find your inability to always use the correct Italian word or phrase frustrating at times, but don't worry too much if this happens. Remember always:

Nothing much ever happens without some effort being made!

On a lighter note, I have to admit to sometimes inventing a 'new' Italian verb or two of my own when finding myself struggling to find the correct Italian version during a conversation! This often leads to a look of consternation on the part of the Italian receiver of my feeble attempt at adding to the already crowded list of verbs used in his or her language.

If you cannot spend time in Italy

While it would be an ideal plan to spend at least some time living and studying in Italy, for most adult students such an attractive arrangement will not be a practical or financial possibility.

If unable to manage the ideal way of proceeding further in your Italian studies, do not despair. As already explained, there are other practical ways open to you by which to make progress. Other that, there is the possibility that you are lucky enough to have a locally based Italian relative, friend or partner who is happy to spend time providing you with assistance and encouragement.

If limited to undertaking all your language studies in your home country, without assistance from a close Italian friend, making the progress necessary to reach your goal will just take a little longer.

I repeat once again, do not let anyone tell you that it is possible to learn to speak Italian following a few months' attendance at a local Italian language school. It is impossible for any normal adult, even a school-age student, to take in and hold sufficient in the way of Italian vocabulary – or confidence with its use in conversation within such a short time. Learning to speak Italian, even over a longer period will not arrive as soon as you may wish, if it is your intention only to attend a classroom-based language course, once or twice per week.

The trick here is to advance beyond the earlier stages of your classroom-based training programme by the additional application of at least some form of aid-assisted self-tuition. Later in this book you will find details of the different kinds of learning aids and various forms of practice that are readily available to you, many via the Internet, others needing to be self-created. A selection of these will offer a practical way of extending and augmenting your level of Italian acquisition. You might also decide to try some of the learning aids and other kinds of activities similar to those I found to be of assistance and continue to use.

As a general rule, having undertaken around six solid months and possibly more of basic Italian with a local language school, you will then need to seriously consider the value of branching out and graduating to the use of a much broader range of self-imposed learning activities. A process of learning best conducted outside the usual style of classroom-based tuition.

The real need from here on in is to achieve a more comprehensive grasp of conversational Italian. This aspect of your learning you will find to be quite a lot different to the more academically structured tuition, the kind usually built around the teaching of grammar and book based texts.

Learning to speak Italian depends more on the capacity of each person to become more directly involved with their learning programme. The example provided earlier in which the learning of conversational Italian was compared with the learning of music bears repeating:

> Learning scripted responses in foreign languages encourages a false sense of confidence. It doesn't translate into real-time speaking competence nor will you understand the musicality of the language. It's like looking at a musical score and expecting to be a master violinist just because you have memorised the notes. Instead you have to play it, and play it again and again. Likewise with the Italian language.
>
> Play with it! Practice! Listen to native Italian speak-

ers and mimic them. Laugh at yourself trying to pronounce "gli" correctly. Italian, more so than many languages, is musical, and if you remember that analogy it will come easier.

It is all very well learning grammar, a host of verbs and other important stuff, but when it comes to the 'music' of Italian, in other words its spoken form, the need now is more toward one of speaking it and playing with it, time and time again, over and over again. You can actually do so out loud, in the street, park, even when retiring to bed – or wherever else you happen to find yourself at the time.

I am aware that some language teachers and others involved with the running of the more generally recognised form of school-based language classes may well disagree with me on this point. I may well have agreed with them, had the subject of learning to speak Italian been discussed some years in the past, before the ready availability of a wide variety of creative learning aids came within every Italian students' grasp.

These days the Internet has opened up a vast new world of information and learning systems – so much so that with their judicious selection and use, any individual can now access most of the material and learning aids needed, to gain the more advanced kind of thinking and speaking skills sought.

Only when I began seriously to look for an alternative means of acquiring Italian did a search start to reveal the wide range of learning aids and other sources of useful information the Internet could provide. Not only that, but following a great deal of research, followed by the practical application of one or two selected aids, I began to find it both possible and practical to devise for myself the system I refer to here as self-tuition.

Organising your self-study programme

Should you decide to go ahead with the concept of self-tuition as described, the basis of your advanced programme of study would normally be expected to comprise a selection of two kinds of activities.

The first of these should be in the form of some kind of audio programme – a format that can be used as the basis of a daily schedule of interactive speaking practices. This should also be supplemented wherever possible with a parallel form of verbal practice – in this case exercises in which as much as possible of the vocabulary being learned is put to use, in a number of different ways.

A single, well-designed audio-based learning system, when combined with a well-written grammar textbook should provide a firm basis for ongoing efforts to extend your range of retained Italian vocabulary.

The amount of time you can spend each day as you augment your studies is of importance here. Unless able to maintain the consistency of your studies to an optimum level, whatever you may learn from here on could well be lost or finish up getting filed away somewhere in the back of your brain, where it is difficult to rediscover later without a great deal of extra effort.

By all means, continue to attend classes at an Italian language school – should you feel this to be necessary. Once started on your self-study programme though, you may find as I did, that both it and other components of your programme can provide all the language practice needed.

The use of textbooks

There are a number of older but reasonably priced printed textbooks that are still in use and available on the market. The type and range of textbooks used by school-based Italian language courses vary, depending on the individual language school's preferences. Most schools insist on their students' use of the course's preferred textbooks. These usually approach the subject of Italian grammar by the inclusion of a combination of text, photographs and in some cases drawings or even cartoons, all in one way or another designed to describe and demonstrate the range of everyday situations with which a student will experience, if and when they eventually visit Italy.

Details of some textbooks are included in the References section.

Audio, radio and newspapers

While in Australia, I regularly use audio as the basis of my regular study programme.

There are a number of audio courses currently available, some via the Internet and others on sale in language bookshops. Some of these are also linked to reading material. The course I eventually selected as the basis for my studies followed a great deal of research. It is a multi-level programme originally developed by Paul Pimsleur,[6] a language teacher well known and

---

[6] "Paul Pimsleur (October 1927–June 1976) was a scholar in the field of applied linguistics. He developed the Pimsleur language learning system, which, along with his many publications, had a significant effect upon theories of language learning and teaching." (Source: Wikipedia)

highly regarded among the international language-teaching fraternity over the years.

This aural + text course is currently distributed under the Pimsleur brand by the US-based Simon & Schuster Company. The full series of 'Pimsleur', a course which ranges over five levels, from basic to advanced, is currently being promoted on the Internet under the heading "How to learn a foreign language" (see References section). The full range of Pimsleur system disc sets are also readily available in most cities from major bookstores and language specific bookshops.

The beauty of using this kind of addition to your self-study programme is that with the discs supplied, or if you have downloaded the programme directly onto your computer, laptop, iPhone, iPad or other similar cellular device, it becomes possible to listen to and interact with its content at any time, day or night, whenever you find yourself with time to spare.

I keep a downloaded version of the total Pimsleur programme on my iPhone, usually listening to and interacting with it during at least one full thirty-minute session each morning. This is often followed by another session in the afternoon or evening, if time permits.

The full Pimsleur programme comprises fifteen hours of language tuition at each of the five levels, of which one of the thirty, thirty-minute sessions is presented in the form of a series of texts. These run parallel to the audio provided within each level.

The Pimsleur programme provides a series of well-presented interactive sessions, each one gradually increasing in scope and difficulty. I regularly combine a lower-level session with a higher-level one, which enables a review of earlier sessions while moving forward to those more advanced in content.

Having a constantly available and easily portable form of study such as this is very practical. It provides a valuable extra dimension to any student's education programme. For example, it provides the flexibility of being ready to use in any number of situations and at different periods of the day – all at times to suit a student's daily schedule.

The additional value offered with this form of study is that it is flexible, best used to advantage whenever the student using it is not expecting to be involved in a conversation – or interacting directly with other human beings.

The point here is that whether the Pimsleur system or some other similar style of audio-based language course you can access and feel comfortable using, this style of learning aid will provide an easily accessible tool that can be used in any number of different locations.

Variety, here, is the spice of life. By that, I mean that in addition to the use of a course similar to Pimsleur, I also find it useful to mix my interactive audio/text studies with a form of self-discussion. In other words, this is the gentle art of 'conducting an intelligent conversation with oneself'. Once you get started with a similar kind of learning aid and get used to the process, you will find that it becomes another valuable tool, particularly when practicing the use of Italian.

I continue to emphasise here that **nothing** can compare with regular, daily attention being given to your study regime, all the time putting as much effort possible into practice, using the language being learned. It would, of course, be preferable if we were living in a real Italian environment in Italy itself, but as that cannot be arranged – you, like me, will need to find other means by which to create as near a learning environment as possible to that you would expect to find in Italy.

Did I sense you thinking that to do so would be difficult or perhaps impossible? I of course will agree that it will be difficult to try to recreate an Italian street scene in either of Melbourne, Sydney, Auckland, New York or London. If however, any progress is to be achieved as a result of our studies, it is essential sometimes that we try to use our imagination by endeavouring to create one!

Imagination can be a fine tool – all that is needed is for us to try to regain a skill we all possessed in some measure, at some stage in our lives, particularly during the years of our childhood. The problem here is that as we grew into becoming adults, many of us seem to have lost much of our earlier ability to imagine! We must try to recapture that and create something that may well exist only in our minds, an imaginary world outside what is considered real and normal.

If you find this difficult to do then perhaps it may be possible for you to practice your Italian among a local group of Italian friends or relatives, even fellow students wishing to practice their language skills, of which there are known to be a few such groups. Groups like these sometimes manage to get together to practice their Italian conversation skills.

It may be that interaction with a group of Italian speakers, and/or keeping in touch with the language via a relative or friend, particularly the former, is not always possible. If so, like me you will just have to use your imagination and make do with every other opportunity that comes along to think about, use, listen to or read Italian.

If you cannot locate such a group, and even if you can, why not try talking to yourself? A good way of doing this is to have a chat with the person that you are always guaranteed to find when looking into your bathroom or hall mirror.

They cannot answer you back, nor can they offer anything in the way of being critical of your Italian grammar. I will later suggest another, much more effective form of self-discussion.

At home in Australia, which of necessity I find myself for most of each year, I listen occasionally to the local Italian radio station *Rete Italia*.

Rete Italia is part of the Italian Media Corporation, an Australian company that publishes both the *Il Globo* and *La Fiamma* newspapers.

Rete Italia broadcasts on a frequency of 1593 kHz, to local Italian speakers in Melbourne, every weekday from 09.00 through to 15.00. At the time of writing, similar programmes are known to operate in Sydney 1539kHz, Brisbane 1053kHz, Adelaide 1629kHz, Perth 657kHz and Darwin 1611kHz.

While still only able to understand parts of the *Rete Italia* radio broadcasts, I am finding that the more I listen, the more I am slowly able to absorb and hold parts of the language being broadcast. Here again it is a slow, gradual often frustrating process.

People who have spent some, if not all of their lives in Australia are usually those responsible for presenting the programmes being broadcast on local *Rete Italia* radio stations throughout the country. Being so, on occasions they may sometimes tend to mingle their Italian with a little colloquial English, or even one or two Anglicised Italian words. One or two sometimes speak at a more moderate pace to that of broadcasters in Italy and this can make the local broadcast a little easier to follow. You too should try it, but only once having advanced well past the intermediate level in your Italian studies.

Another 'trick' I have found to be of help is listening to my Pimsleur audio sessions in bed at night. When at home I have been known to retire to bed with a pair of Bluetooth ear buds plugged in each ear, listening and interacting with a selection of recorded Italian sessions by Pimsleur, leaching into my brain. Once or twice, I have actually fallen asleep during the process.

That, you might say, is taking things a bit too far, but when you come to consider the usefulness of utilising any opportunity and any quiet period when alone and in a relaxed state, during which to advance progress with your language learning, sometimes even an hour or so of study before sleep can be of benefit.

Being relaxed in bed before dropping off to sleep often does the trick for me. I have found for example, that I seem to retain more in the way of the more difficult kinds of vocabulary by listening while I am in a relaxed state before sleep.

Why not try listening in bed yourself? This is with the proviso, of course, that your spouse or current sleeping partner has no objection to such a possibly disruptive intrusion into your relationship!!

I sometimes purchase a copy of the local Melbourne-based Italian newspaper *Il Globo*. I try to read as much as I can but still find much of the text difficult to understand. Persistence though is the name of the game here, so I keep trying, along with the assistance of my trusty English/Italian dictionary. It sometimes helps a little if you try reading an article referring to a local issue, something that you have some knowledge of.

As you become more 'educated' with your Italian, you will

eventually find yourself better able to 'read-between-the-lines' and while doing so you will soon find yourself getting better at piecing together what is being reported. Finding yourself able to achieve even this level is a good indication that your Italian comprehension is well on the road to improving.

The message here is to take heart, at least in the knowledge that your improving ability to decipher what you are reading is an indicator of your continuing progress toward a degree of fluency. It is a case of *poco a poco* (little by little) – one step at a time is the name of the game!

As a final comment on the relationships seen to exist between an individual's capacity to read and speak Italian, I can do no better than include a section from among the Pimsleur audio programme's guidance notes:

> Reading has been defined as "decoding graphic material to determine its message". To put it another way, reading consists of coming back to speech through its graphic symbols. In short, meanings reside in the sounds of the spoken language. **Speaking a language is the necessary first step to acquiring the ability to read a language and understanding its meaning.**

And if one is a little older?

It is generally recognised that the older one gets, trying to learn something new, whether a new language or a new skill, indeed anything complex and different from what any individual has been used to doing, thinking or their way of speaking for the greater part of their life, gets to be more difficult. Young children, on the other hand, who have absorbed little information and are not as yet totally indoctrinated or educated in all the stuff that they are being influenced to absorb during their early years, are a little different when it come to learning a second language.

Disciplines like schoolwork, parental attitudes, religion and social values aside, young children of a migrant family that has a different language to their host country are known to find the learning of a second street or school language, in addition to one being used at home, easier than their parents might.

Children of such a family will usually find their new environment relatively easy to accommodate. They will usually become able with little apparent effort to get to grips with their new language as they bond with newly found street and school friends. Their parents on the other hand will more than likely find moving from one language to another much more challenging.

9. Some answers and activities

You should have gathered by now that there really is no sure-fire shortcut to learning Italian as a second language, but do not allow yourself to be put off by that.

With dedication to the task, the use of an appropriate range of learning aids on a regular daily basis, plus at least a few months prior of Italian classes at a reputable language school to get yourself started on the right track, you should now be in a good position to progress toward achieving your aim of becoming a reasonably competent speaker of Italian.

Hopefully later, you may be able to travel to and spend time in Italy, where you may well surprise yourself with the amount of Italian vocabulary you have already absorbed thus far – without realising it!

Try to spend some time in Italy

Why not go ahead with the idea firmly planted in your mind that the time will eventually arrive enabling you to make that dreamed-of visit to Italy?

I realise that while a visit to Italy would be the ideal way by which to gain much more from your Italian studies, it may well be currently beyond your current financial capacity, difficult to slot into a busy working year or fit in among family commitments. Don't give up thoughts of doing so just yet though, you never know what the next week or year might bring.

Having said that, without any doubt the best way to learn any new language and gain the most out of using it once having become familiar with its grammar and having managed to obtain a wide range of vocabulary, is to become involved in the country's day-to-day life, hearing the language being used every day.

When you do eventually get to make the trip and having earlier decided to try always to use whatever level of Italian you have managed to amass, you will gradually find yourself increasingly capable of leaving behind the need of always having to convert what it is that you want to communicate, from English.

Doing something along this line, providing of course that you have earlier taken the trouble to learn and absorb a broad enough range of Italian vocabulary, will be sufficient to get you started.

You won't need to delve into a tense known as *passato remoto* (verbs relating to events in the more remote past) or even, particularly during the earlier stages, have the need to master some of what are sometimes known as 'compound tenses'.

The different ways in which various verb forms need to be linked when discussing a variety of differing situations is more advanced and can prove difficult to remember which combinations to use, and where, during any conversation.

Another aspect of Italian grammar that can be difficult to remember is the choice of which form of the various verbs to use in a given situation, for example: *dovere* (have to/need to/shall) or *potere* (could/be able to/might). The correct selection between these could prove difficult at first – that is, until one is able to get an as yet uneducated brain and tongue around deciding on the appropriate verb form to use during the course of any conversation one becomes engaged in.

Ask a lot of questions

If you do eventually get to visit Italy, you should arrive there prepared to force yourself into situations where you need to ask questions. Don't be afraid to do so.

If necessary, tell whomever you are speaking to at the time that you are a visitor and you are trying to improve your Italian. Try saying this in Italian.

Rest assured that any native Italian would know that you are a *straniero/a* (stranger) without you even telling them, just as soon as they clap eyes on you. That fact will register with them well before you even begin to open your mouth and your overloaded brain starts preparing itself, before trying to put into words what it is that you think you might be wanting or needing to say.

You will soon find that just the act of trying to converse in Italian, regardless of the level of your current capacity will be accepted.

Make a note to show anyone with whom you get into a conversation with, that you wish to pay them the compliment of learning and using your Italian when visiting their beautiful country, and of course while addressing them.

Don't be afraid to go into a shop or supermarket to buy, or even better perhaps, why not try to barter for something using your hard gained Italian? You will find that some Italian traders love to barter. Only by forcing yourself to do everyday things like that will you really begin to feel the benefit of improvement across your range of learned vocabulary.

The more effort you put in trying to speak Italian, the more confidence you will gather, both with your Italian comprehension and your capacity to carry on a reasonably intelligent conversation. After all, isn't that the aim of the many months, perhaps years of study that you have put in, just to reach such a desirable situation? Think about it – just experiencing the joy of being in Italy and finding yourself able to speak Italian.

Sometimes you will find that when you start to speak in Italian to a shopkeeper, waiter, hotel receptionist or some other local you have just met, they may well try to help you by replying to you in English. Should this occur, and it will occur often, particularly when you are checking into a hotel or entering a restaurant and wish to see the menu or need to order pre-dinner drinks. It is important to always try speaking in Italian. Your intent and insistence on using Italian will always be appreciated and accepted.

Accept that the level of your conversation at first will be limited, so that you cannot really expect to engage in a deeper, more philosophical or technical discussion like you can in your native English. Nevertheless, if you persist you will find that gradually, more and more vocabulary will open up to you, much in the manner of a slowly opening window.

Some people will have a greater possibility to learn a new language quicker than others. But don't hold back, just go for it and make your mistakes. **Mistakes will happen anyway, and it really doesn't matter!**

Comment

Remember one thing more. Learning to speak Italian is not all that different from the time you learned to swim, or ride a bike. Well, perhaps not exactly the same – learning Italian will need more in the way of study and effort, and it usually takes a little longer.

Try 'letting go of the bar'

Do you remember that special day when, having learned the necessary swimming strokes, you finally gathered up enough courage and decided to let go of the bar at the side of the local swimming pool for the very first time?

Putting your fears to the back of your mind, you probably took a deep breath, then with heart thumping against your ribs you finally found the courage to plunge and splash into your first desperate swimming strokes, finally arriving successfully, though perhaps not as elegantly as you would have wished, at the other side of the pool, exhausted but feeling supreme! Well, it's just the same as that with learning Italian – but with less chance of getting wet!

The time will eventually arrive during your Italian studies when you will also need to allow yourself to let yourself go, splashing out, perhaps a little ungainly at first, as you enter into the exciting world of spoken Italian. I think you will get my drift here.

Remember also that it can be great fun in the doing, and there is not the least possible danger of drowning!

If you do get the opportunity to travel to Italy, try to extend your stay for a week or so longer than originally intended, preferably using the early part of your visit to enrol in a local language school. Do so even if it is for just one or possibly two full weeks of local tuition.

You will find there are a number of local Italian language schools you can enrol in. I found one such local school purely by accident, which turned out to be really good, purely by accident.

I just happened to find *Euro Studi Veneto* while surfing the Internet and trying to locate a locally based language school, preferably one within easy reach of where I intended to stay for three months during the summer of 2015.

The school's website looked interesting, offering a variety of course levels. Student groups, I was interested to note, would be kept small enough to ensure that each person received personal attention to their particular needs, and that suited me.

I found it very useful to learn on enquiry, that while based on assisting the acquisition and correct use of Italian grammar, the school's tutoring programme included a great deal of practice with conversational Italian. This proved to be so later, students being encouraged to participate regularly in discussion that closely involved tutors and students on various topical subjects.

There will of course be other language schools of a similar nature to be found in various cities around Italy, but try to ensure that the number of students expected to be included in any such course that looks to be interesting is limited to around eight, preferably less – unlike the course I attended at the *Universita per Stranieri* in Perugia.

Contact information and other details for *E.STI.VE Euro Studi Veneto* is included in the References section.

10. Putting things together

To repeat yet again ... "Learning to speak Italian will take effort, time and patience". Do not expect to be speaking Italian after just a few short lessons, or even following some months of study. Certainly, it will not happen following months and months of academically oriented study at a local language school.

Learning a second language will require a lot of personal effort and many hours of study and practice, with concentration later being focused on the use of your Italian vocabulary.

Another important aspect of learning, particularly during the early stages, is the need to pay close attention when observing and practicing how the individual letters in the Italian alphabet sound and are spoken, how Italian words are pronounced and how the language is constructed and used on a daily basis by native Italian speakers.

The most critical stage in the learning process arrives much later, usually when you are beginning to find yourself starting to come up against one or other of the barriers discussed earlier. You should by then have also concluded that something relating to the kind of training being currently accessed needs to change. That will also be the time when it should have become clear that a more advanced set of skills are needed if you are to progress further toward gaining the capacity to maintain a conversation in Italian.

You have now arrived at the point where your ability to

speak and the dexterity with which your brain reacts now requires a different form of stimulation.

Being older, particularly having spent the greater part of your life to date thinking, reading and communicating solely in English will make the skills needed a little more difficult to acquire – even more so if undertaking language studies part-time.

You also need to be **realistic**. Do not expect to make progress toward your goal without being prepared to put in the extra effort required. **It won't just happen – you need to make it happen!**

As Italian is your language of choice, by all means start by attending one or other of the local Italian courses being run in or around your city. A quick search on the Internet will enable you to locate an appropriate course.

Give preference to those courses being run by, native Italian-speaking teachers, people who are fully qualified to teach.

If possible, choose a course that includes a growing component of Italian conversation practice in its more advanced stages. Recognise always that everyone starting out on the road to learning Italian will eventually need to absorb a wide range of vocabulary, sufficient at least to enable you to take part in an 'everyday' level of conversation.

It's all very well being able to tell someone: "my name is Peter" in Italian, or some other similarly short phrase, but it will take a lot more hard work to enable you to extend yourself very far beyond that.

As you progress beyond the intermediate stages of your studies, you will find that your expanding range of Italian vocabulary will gradually enable you to extend the range of conversation and reading that you will be able to achieve. This will usually take a little time. So be patient and:

Keep practicing, repeating, listening and practicing, over and over, on a regular basis. While doing so, don't be afraid to make mistakes because you will make plenty of them, believe me!

U3A's Italian language programme

I am including a few lines here to discuss the U3A programme, as it could be of interest to any senior members of the community seeking to take up Italian studies.

If one is among the growing number of those regarded by society as nearing or having become what is known of these days as a 'Senior Citizen', as a first step toward the gaining of an initial level of grammar in a language other then English, you could try the U3A programme (University of the 3rd Age).

Italian courses are run by U3A in various locations across the country. While unable to offer expertise and language tuition of a similar standard to CIS and similarly specialised language schools, U3A is a reasonably good place at which to make a start. Another advantage of the U3A programme is that it is distributed widely across many local suburban areas of Australia's major cities and major provincial population centres.

U3A offers a variety of forums for discussion and learning – among the latter, languages. In Australia, there are a number of active U3A groups, based in each state of the Commonwealth each local group offering courses to its members, across a broad range of subjects.

In Victoria, as part of my research for this book, I joined

U3A's Frankston branch and enrolled in the intermediate level Italian course being provided at its campus there.

The course was being run by a capable tutor, not a native Italian, but sufficiently versed in Italian grammar and possessing a good range of conversational Italian to provide members of her group with a programme of interesting and useful Italian studies. These ranged from basic, up to what could be regarded as reasonably close to or just below intermediate level.

The main limitation of the U3A Italian language programme that I attended was that it comprised a relatively large group of students. It also became obvious that most of the attendees appeared more interested in the social aspects of the course being presented. This tended to limit the level to which the course could take a student, at least one seriously wishing to become a reasonably capable Italian speaker.

This is not a criticism of what turned out to be a well run and resourced series of interactive sessions. Such a course in fact could be of some assistance to an older beginner, someone wishing to gain some knowledge of Italian, while at the same time gaining some useful insights into Italian culture.

Regardless of where you decide to start your quest to become an Italian speaker, it is important to make sure that any classes or courses that you are planning to attend, have the minimum of students involved – preferably less than eight if that can be managed, even better if fewer than that.

The U3A course I attended regularly had between ten and fourteen older students in attendance at any one time. This tended to restrict the capacity of the tutor, the course running for only a couple of hours on a once-weekly basis, to give more than very basic attention to any one student, or subject.

Taking up any course with a lesser number of students may

well mean a higher cost, but if you are serious it will be well worth considering.

Have a look also at one or other of the better-known aural/written courses, similar to the Pimsleur audio series described earlier. Use of this or something similar will, if worked with consistently, serve to assist you to extend your range and capacity to retain learned Italian vocabularies, starting from the very basic, up to advanced level.

Also important is the need to practice and if possible, to adopt the correct way that a word or phrase should be spoken (pronunciation). Listening and repeating phrases and words as presented in one or other of the aural tapes and similar aids referred to in this guide will assist here.

As you progress beyond intermediate level, try also to listen as often as possible to an Italian radio programme being broadcast in your city or town. Even though you may find a great deal of difficulty with understanding all that is being said, you will find some words or phrases you can recognise, particularly as you advance with your regular daily spoken language workouts.

Regular reading of Italian texts will also go a long way toward assisting you to gradually add to your vocabulary. This is in addition to advancing your understanding of how the general structure of written Italian differs from your native English.

As a learner, it is not recommended that you even attempt to read works written by Dante Alighieri, Italy's claimed equivalent of England's Shakespeare. Few native Italian speakers even try.

By all means, occasionally purchase a copy of one or other of *Il Globo* or *La Fiamma*. Both are locally produced Italian newspapers in Australia. Try reading the paper using your English/Italian dictionary. You will need it, I can assure you. Even then, you will often find a large gap between your understanding of some individual words, and the gist of what the article you are trying to read is saying.

As suggested earlier, you should consider the purchase of one or two books written for younger Italians. The language used and concepts discussed with publications like these are usually more simply stated and therefore should prove easier for a foreign student of Italian to understand.

Buy a good book on Italian grammar

There are a large number of publications discussing Italian grammar available either in printed form or via the Internet. Most of these will be of some assistance throughout your study programme.

I use a relatively older, hardback textbook, written and published by Ferruccio Komadina and Giuseppe Orifici, both from the University of Western Australia. This particular text was first published in 1969 under the title: *A Progressive Italian Grammar*.

My copy has been well thumbed from constant use. This book was first published some 45 years ago with a number of later updates and reprints. Having, from time to time, invested in other books on Italian grammar published much later, I found this particular textbook proved more useful to me, particularly because of the way in which its content was presented by its Italian authors.

The book has been revised and re-issued a number of times, the latest I understand being in 1995 – a significant comment perhaps on its popularity and perceived value to many other students of Italian over the years. I have seen copies of the book still being offered for sale in pre-owned bookshops and I believe second-hand copies are still being advertised on one or two Internet sites.

By all means, try working with different kinds of textbooks, and while you are at it, research and possibly try out a selection of other teaching aids, with the aim of finding that which best suits your particular way of learning. Doing so will be worth the cost. Remember also that most people have their preferred way of learning, so it pays to experiment to find what proves best for you.

Once having found the range and kind of aids that suit your way of studying and you feel comfortable with, use them on a regular basis, committing yourself to some study and practice for at least an hour, preferably two – Every day if possible.

Don't be afraid to talk to yourself

I discussed doing something like this a little earlier. Perhaps the suggestion sounds just a little odd at first? I know that I often receive some strange looks as passers-by hear me diligently practicing having a conversation with myself in Italian.

Talking to oneself is a great way of having a conversation in any language. If you think about it – we all do it from time to time when alone, so it's nothing new or radically different to what we know and do already. The process is sort of similar to a chess player playing both sides of the chessboard, only a little louder.

When out and about – preferably alone, try discussing with yourself what you see around you, in Italian of course. Also try to discuss what you are doing, what you are thinking of doing for the rest of the day, what you plan to do tomorrow or even perhaps, also for a change, what you did yesterday and why? Practice the range of Italian vocabulary that you will be expecting to use in general conversation later, in the various tenses:

- The present
- The past (*passato prossimo*)
- The future
- The conditional

Why not try conducting an imaginary conversation with yourself? If doing so be careful to talk to yourself discretely as you never know who might be listening as you pass them by, deeply engrossed and seemingly oblivious to everything going on around you.

While we are on the subject of talking to yourself, I recall an occasion in Melbourne earlier this year that found me standing in front of a shoe shop in Elizabeth Street in Melbourne's CBD, while I conducted a discussion with myself in Italian on the subject of which shoes I liked, and why. I suddenly realised that a couple standing next to me were giving me some strange looks, probably trying to make sense of what their neighbour was rabbiting on about, and in a foreign language!

Don't be put off with what people might think or say and don't pass up any opportunity to chat, even with yourself, if you can't find anyone else to talk to in Italian. Remember also that it makes for very good practice.

If doing so, it will pay to have a pocket version of Italian verbs or have an English/Italian translation app installed on your cell phone. I have two free Internet-based translation apps on my iPhone, one titled "Babylon", the other "iTranslate". There are other such services and most of them are free. Such a handy and easy to access translation service can be a useful tool to have around, particularly when you are out and about and cannot remember the Italian word you need.

Once having found the word or remembered the phrase you were seeking continue to weave a conversation around it. Alternatively, try to develop a sentence or two using it – then repeat the phrase for a few minutes. This will assist you to recall it later. Remember, it's all very good fun as well as being instructive. Strange as it may seem at first, the process actually works – if you keep at it!!

And now that you are thinking along a new line of attack, why not try to do some counting and telling the time in Italian? Doing so is relatively easy to get to grips with. Once you get yourself going, you will gradually find it easier to switch over to using Italian instead of always counting in English. Once again, it's very good practice!

Why not also try counting the steps when ascending or descending a staircase, and why not practice addition and subtraction in Italian? Yes, of course that will prove to be a little more difficult but why not try it just the same?

It's also good fun trying to work out what you are paying for something when doing the daily shopping, but instead of thinking it out in English, try to calculate both it and your expected change in Italian? Of course doing stuff like that noted above will be difficult at first, but you will be surprised how quickly things will begin to click. Take the trouble to get yourself into the knack of doing something similar, every time you get the opportunity.

Don't worry too much if someone next to you starts to give you a strange look, in such cases I just smile and usually trot out a happy *buon giorno* (good day), and keep on going.

While on the subject of talking and calculating for yourself in Italian, if you do happen to meet up with an Italian speaker while out and about in your home city or town, try getting into some sort of conversation with them. It would be useful, of course, to first advise them that you are trying to learn the language. This could be important in ensuring that they don't get the wrong idea about your intentions and reason for 'chatting them up'!

You never know when you will get an opportunity to practice your Italian on another human being. When the opportunity does come your way – grab hold of it with both hands. Believe me, opportunities to practice can occur, some in the strangest of places.

An example of this which recently came my way, found me sitting on a city-bound tram in North Melbourne on my way into the Melbourne CBD. At the time I was, as per usual, muttering to myself in what I hoped was reasonably correct Italian, trying as I then was to describe a passing car and whether I liked it or not.

You can imagine my surprise on hearing the elderly gentleman sitting next to me on the tram turn to me and ask "*Lei Italiano?*" (Are you Italian?). Taken aback somewhat by his unexpected question, once I got my brain into gear I explained that I was learning Italian and was just practicing. He laughed, complimented me for the effort, following which we then struck up a conversation (in Italian of course) that lasted all the way into the city, whereupon I invited him to join me in a nearby café for what turned out to be a passable cappuccino and stale brioche.

What followed was an interesting hour with my new acquaintance, conducted mostly in Italian. My companion would have already known from my accent as soon as I got to open my mouth and well before we even got started, that I obviously wasn't Italian.

During our conversation I learned that at the time he was on his way into the city from his home in North Melbourne, with no special plans other than just to spend a couple of hours wandering around the shops, as well as taking a cup of coffee. He found himself instead unexpectedly tutoring me in his beautifully delivered Standard Italian. He told me later that he was a retired teacher! So there you go – how lucky can you get?

My only regret is that in my excitement following our coffee and chat together, then needing to rush off to catch my train home, I neglected to ask him if he would be interested to perhaps meet me week in town next week for a coffee and chat.

I have since caught the same tram from time to time after visiting my son Leon, who was at the time working in a popular Arden Street café in North Melbourne, but have yet to meet up with my Italian tutor – at least to date but … I am still hoping.

Why not consider a language course in Italy?

Of course I realise that not everyone can, or is even interested to the extent that they plan to visit Italy for more time than it takes to visit one or even more places of interest there – even if they could afford the time and expense involved.

But think about it. Perhaps if you are thinking of taking a cruise on one or other of those big, white 'Floating Dream Palaces' (generally known in the shipping trade as luxury cruise ships), for the doubtful privilege of being shunted from port to port on board a big ship filled to almost brimming with people, why not try visiting Italy and try instead to learn some Italian?

Some vacationers, having taking up what on the surface appear to be very attractive offers from the various cruise ship operators, may be heard to claim with pride that they are regular 'Cruisers'. Having so described themselves, they can also be expected to trot out a bunch of boring photos of the big ship they spent some days weeks or months on board recently, as they ate, cocktailed, snacked and gorged their way across one or more of the world's oceans.

You instead might find it interesting just to try something different, another form of overseas travel perhaps? This could be a vacation that would certainly prove far more beneficial to your ongoing mental health and feelings of real, solid and long lasting achievement.

I find it difficult to understand what real value to one's life is gained by regularly booking on one or other of those big ships, wherein all anyone can really do for most of each day is sit around, or drink, eat or gamble oneself into a potential bad state of health. Perhaps try it once, but surely not every year?

Why expose yourself to the distinct possibility of catching some virulent bug, virus or worse from someone or other from among the couple of thousand other people milling around the daily food courts and restaurants, or from being sneezed at and coughed on in one of the many bars and overcrowded theatres. Passengers to be found at every turn, literally brushing shoulders and everything else together, as you all meander around and around the ship.

Cruising may also expose you to a regularly reported shipboard malady, one that seems to be reoccurring with monotonous regularity these days – in the form of a variety of gastric conditions and premature deaths, the latter usually and thankfully restricted to one or two among the more elderly cruisers.

Before writing a book on the subject, I decided to experience what being cooped up inside the hull of a large, luxuriously appointed cruise ship would actually be like. This mode of travel, incidentally, seemed to get smaller and more cramped the longer I remained on board, regardless of the size of the ship I was on.

Perhaps instead, why not consider a few weeks visiting Venice, Treviso, Sicily, Sorrento, Rome, Naples, Lake Como, Lake Garda, Perugia and/or a few other really interesting locations around beautiful Italy, while at the same time brushing up on your Italian?

I am certain that such a plan would prove much more beneficial, both to your health and, if the earlier reported findings of various universities is anything to go by, also your long-term mental wellbeing. So, why not think about it?

Please excuse this minor diversion from the main theme of this book. It had occurred to me during its writing that life could be so much richer and healthier if more cruisers decided instead to spend a month or so visiting some part of Italy, during which time they might also undertake some Italian language or combined language, art or cooking classes, or even perhaps to join a walking tour in the Dolomites or Sicily.

As you are reading this, I am guessing that you are already interested in either learning or improving your Italian. That being the case, comparing the advantages on offer by taking a vacation in Italy as against one of cruising on a big white ship is probably irrelevant.

Speaking Italian – In Italy

I have reached the stage in my quest to improve my spoken Italian where, in spite of the obvious difficulties I still face – which happily seem to be getting less the longer and harder I study and practice – I can do most of the things I need to do when visiting Italy.

I have not achieved anywhere near the required 10,000 hours of study and practice noted earlier and in the References section to follow. Even though I am sometimes able to spend less than ten hours a week on my Italian studies here in Australia, I am progressing with serious intent toward what I hope to be a reasonably proficient communicator in Italian.

Sometimes I find myself falling back a couple of steps along the way, sometimes forgetting what I had learned last week or even yesterday. Gradually, though, I am finding myself able to pick up and progress beyond where I was a month or so ago.

I still manage to forget words and other important stuff, but all things being equal I am progressing. Even at my level of a kind of semi-fluency, when last in Italy I found booking into a hotel or discussing prices in a shop, at a market or wherever else I happened to be at the time presented no real difficulties.

At times I still falter and find myself stuttering when trying to find the correct words or phrase to use. But on the whole I can communicate all the necessary information needed, even if doing so takes a little longer than I would like and even if what I was trying to say resulted in something a little different to the way a native Italian would say it.

While I am in Italy, I enjoy wandering around bookshops and pushing myself into a conversation with the owner, perhaps to discuss a book and its author or just to pass the time practicing my hard gained Italian. I also find it interesting to wander around the local supermarket during a shopping trip, sometimes asking for assistance from one or other of the staff, or even one or two of the local shoppers.

I enjoy visiting boutiques, bars, markets and any other interesting place where people usually gather, to practice and sometimes test myself, always in the knowledge that I can just about cope with a two-way conversation with any considerate native Italian, should they be happy to spend a few minutes indulging a visitor to their city or township.

Having reached that point, however, I realise that I have much more to learn and practice before I can lay claim to being anywhere near fluent.

I find it difficult when trying to switch from English, at a time when I have been working on my next book (written in English of course) or following an English conversation.

It is especially difficult when following a conversation with another English speaker I then try to get my brain to switch over to using Italian. Often this results in a period of involuntary panic setting in, a state that then tends to leave my mind blank for a short time, robbing me of the capacity to plunge immediately back into Italian.

It's often encouraging and sometimes amusing, though, when with my Italian *amico* Franco – to hear him assuring me "*Gerry, parli bene l'Italiano*" (you speak Italian well). I know for a fact that he is being kind and reassuring, pleasant and helpful. Really, my Italian – to him, his family, and other Italian friends – must often border on the hilarious!

Having said that, it usually makes little or no difference whatsoever the level of Italian a visitor to Italy can manage when trying desperately to communicate in Italian to an Italian. The considerate local will enjoy the fact that the friend or visitor is at least trying their best to speak well in Italian. Most Italians, faced with a similar situation, will usually seek to be complimentary with the foreign speaker's efforts, even though his or her rendition and pronunciation may well be less than worthy of such a compliment.

Italians will usually appreciate that a mere foreigner has taken the trouble to want to learn and address them in their beautiful language. The fact that you have requested them not to use English, whether a waiter in a bar or restaurant, pizzeria, or even the cashier at the supermarket when she offers a discount voucher with your change and you are able to reply "*grazie ma non posso usarlo, sono un/a visitatore/trice qui*" (thank you but I cannot use it, I am a visitor here), will please them on its own.

If a similar situation occurs during your visit to a supermarket, just take a look around at the queue of people waiting for their turn to pay. Don't be surprised to see a few smiles and perhaps one or two nods of approval being directed toward you for being courteous – and of course in recognition of you attempting to speak reasonably good Italian. This always assumes, of course, that you decide to grab the opportunity to answer in this fashion.

These days I usually accept any supermarket discount voucher being offered, but then will seek to present it to the next person, usually a lady standing in line waiting to pay. Should you too come up against a similar situation, a good plan would be to offer the voucher to the next lady in line with the comment "*per Lei signora, sono un visitatore qui e lasciaro Italia domani*" (I am a visitor here and will be leaving Italy tomorrow). This approach is guaranteed to meet with approval, so don't be surprised if you then receive a heartfelt "*grazie mille*" from the recipient.

Yes, Italians do look forward to receiving discount coupons from the local supermarket, very much so, and much like most shoppers do back in Australia – or anywhere else for that matter.

TIM and my iPhone

If you do decide to spend some time in Italy, it is usually a good plan to purchase a local sim card to fit into your mobile (cell) phone (*telefonino* or *cellulare* in Italian – both descriptions I believe are considered to be masculine, but please don't ask me why). I have asked many times just how a mobile phone came to be regarded as being masculine. To date, no one I have asked seems to know either. I usually get a shrug of the shoulders, a questioning scrunch of the face, and a confused look that seems to say: "I don't really know why, but that is as it is."

Be careful to ensure that you understand the extent of the phone service you have purchased, and don't, like me, sometimes forget when you may need to organise to recharge it, should your stay turn out to be a little longer than the extent of your current arrangements with the local telephone company.

One of the problems a foreign visitor to Italy will find, particularly one who might well speak some Italian, is that they may – like me – still find difficulty when trying to follow the recorded voice message the phone company has sent to their cell phone, advising that time is running out and they need to arrange to recharge their locally purchased sim card.

I don't usually have a problem making sense of any text messages received, advising of my pending need to recharge my phone. On the last occasion however, on dialling the number provided in the text message I failed, no matter how many times I replayed the rapidly spoken message over, to make head or tail of what exactly the phone company message was advising and how I should proceed to organise the recharge.

This eventually decided me to give up trying to understand the phone message. Instead, I paid a visit to the local TIM office *in centro* (city centre/downtown). TIM incidentally is one of Italy's telephone companies, the equivalent of Australia's Telstra.

When I finally made my way from the end of a rather long queue also waiting for technical assistance of some kind or other, I was thankfully capable of explaining to the totally non-English-speaking counter assistant that my Italian was not up to following TIM's recorded message, a message spoken at full *autostrada* (freeway) like speed.

My phone problem took but a few minutes to fix and arrange for the recharging of my sim card. Of course, like everything else in Italy, there was now a long queue similar in size to that which had me waiting there before being served, with even more customers still waiting patiently. Having sorted out my recharge, I was encouraged just to observe the smiles and what I took to be looks of sympathy from other TIM customers, now waiting in line behind me.

It goes to show that it pays to learn sufficient Italian to be capable of getting you by with any sort of problem you may need to seek assistance for while visiting. It also underlines the value of having enough Italian at your disposal to get your message over – even to a non-English-speaking local counter assistant.

This is another example where having the confidence to use whatever level of Italian you have managed to learn, will always make for a more enjoyable experience during your visit.

As already described, there are a variety of ways to improve your knowledge of and capabilities with spoken Italian. It really gets down to a question of your commitment, plus what time you are prepared to put into pursuing your hopes of becoming a competent speaker of Italian.

Incidentally, despite the considered opinions of some of the 'experts', you shouldn't need anything like 10,000 hours of concentrated study to achieve a reasonable and useful level of Italian language capability. You might need between five and ten percent of that number of hours, but not much more.

Whichever course you have started out on or are in the process of continuing, remember that persistence will always pay in the end.

Whenever you find yourself beginning to struggle as you make your way along the road to success:

Don't forget to enjoy the journey!

11. Three months in Treviso – 2015

The earlier part of this book examined some of the main issues expected to confront most adult native English speakers seeking to gain some fluency with spoken Italian.

Also discussed were the circumstances and thinking that led me to look for an alternative route along which to progress. I wanted a way of tuition beyond the scope of the usual format of classroom-based, academic-style teaching that I had been able to access up to that point. I also explained that following some months of language tuition on a once-weekly basis, I was now finding it difficult to advance much further, particularly when trying to extend the level of my Italian language acquisition to include conversational Italian.

Before moving on from this point, it will be useful to expand the narrative I have embarked on thus far a little more – in particular, the part that concerns my experiences with school-based Italian language tuition courses.

It eventually became clear to me that I had reached a point in my Italian studies where I was becoming stalled. Whatever was happening, or rather not happening at the time, was seriously affecting my capacity to gain vocabulary and the confidence to use it.

I had to that time considered myself reasonably intelligent and capable, even when it came to learning a diversity of new, technically involved skills. During a working lifetime, I had also proved myself capable of holding down a number of demanding management positions across a variety of industries, most very different in nature. I had later started up my own business, operating in an industry that had required me to undertake a technically demanding course to gain the necessary technical qualifications.

Why then, when it came to Italian conversation, a subject that seemed from the outside to be reasonably straightforward, apart from the understandably different phonetics, pronunciation and grammar structure involved, was I finding progress beyond my then level so difficult?

When it came to my desire to speak Italian with a reasonable level of clarity and proficiency, I saw no reason why I should be experiencing the level of difficulties I found myself coming up against when trying to advance in that direction.

I recall at the time asking myself the question "Surely there has to be some other means through which I can create a learning environment that can provide me with a more productive path along which to progress?" At the same time, a more creative means of gaining the capacity to think and speak more efficiently in Italian.

The answer I usually received from my school tutors was to continue with my classroom-based studies, in the expectation that with later modules there would be more opportunities to use the language being learned.

The problem with this advice was that when discussing the situation in which I found myself with other students actually attending these so-called 'advanced' language sessions, they usually expressed disappointment with the course they were attending. In particular, they tended to be disappointed with these courses' capacity to significantly improve their ability to think and communicate more confidently with spoken Italian.

This, then, was the main issue that set me along a path that eventually resulted in the programme of self-tuition that I later switched over to and followed for close on a year, which I have endeavoured to describe.

Returning to the present, or at least to June 2015 and my then arrival in Italy with the intention of assessing the success or otherwise of my self-tuition programme. The question that then arose, following a year of independent and relatively inexpensive self-study, was the need to assess whether or not the programme was meeting the objectives I had set a year earlier?

Would my plan to stay longer in Italy answer that question? Had the months of research and later studies and practice development, working on my own, assisted me to gain my goal of at least becoming more conversationally capable, and thus find myself closer to achieving an acceptable level of Italian?

Another important question here was a financial one. While currently retired and a writer of sorts, thus far earning very little from my writing projects, would I be able to organise and finance the projected three-month-long visit, at the same time also arrange to undertake three weeks of prior tuition at a local Italian language school?

Why choose Treviso?

Another question you may well be asking at this point: "What was it that was so special as to convince you to select the ancient city of Treviso as the place to test whether or not your self-study programme was working?"

Without a doubt, within the borders of the Italian peninsula many interesting and historical regions, cities and towns can be found. A number of Italian cities can also lay claim to being the location of a professionally run Italian language school. While this may well be so, I was already familiar with the Veneto region.

During the 1990s and early 2000s I had established a business connection with a company located near Preganziol, a township located several kilometres to the south of Treviso. A number of visits to the company offices there had enabled me to become reasonably familiar with the Veneto region. My chosen location therefore seemed as good as any other.

The more I visited Treviso and the surrounding countryside over following years, the more I became impressed with the variety of attractions – physical, historical and artistic that both the city, its nearby region of the same name and the Veneto province in general had to offer a visitor.

Now, having found what appeared to be a professionally run language school located in the historical centre of Treviso, the decision to make it the place in which to test my project seemed natural. The location also represented an ideal opportunity to travel and absorb more of the history and culture of the region.

I will have a little more to say about this relatively small, historical and appealing city and its features later.

The Veneto province was also the region of Italy where I had established a series of bicycle tours during the early 1990s. The tours had been established in partnership with a local specialist travel agency, operating under the intriguing title of "*Alice Nel Paese Delle Meraviglie*" (Alice in Wonderland). In spite of my limited capacity at the time with the Italian language, I had managed to guide groups of social bike riders from Australia around the province.

The tour was limited to small groups. Members joined me to pedal their way around this varied and undulating region of Italy, which took in some of the more interesting locations across the province. All this was achieved while the group dined each lunchtime and evening on locally produced foods, while savouring wines grown in each location visited, all of which having been selected, prepared and presented by local cooks and chefs.

Having now explained the factors that motivated my three-month-long visit to Italy, June 2015 found me on board a speeding train, north toward Venice. I was now at last on the final leg of a journey that could be regarded as a kind of pilgrimage across the cradle of Italian civilisation, all the way from Melbourne, Australia.

Quasi Trevigiano

In local parlance, my aim now was to become *un quasi Trevigiano* (a part-time resident of Treviso).

Once settled into my temporary home, I planned to shop locally for food and other household needs. I even planned to update what had over the years become a somewhat worn out and out-of-date wardrobe of clothing as a part of the project, thus requiring me to shop and on a number of occasions to negotiate a price for various items for my newly updated wardrobe. I planned also to shop for my grocery needs and do some of my own cooking, eating and drinking *a casa* (at home) in addition to dining out and about at one or other of the local *pizzerie, trattorie* and bars, of which the city and surrounding province were well provided.

My aim on this visit to Italy was to immerse myself totally into life and living Italian-style, even to the extent of trying to develop the capacity to think and adapt myself as much as I could with all things Italian, the language of course being paramount. Now was the time to find out whether or not my concentrated self-tutoring programme for the past year had lived up to my hopes.

For the period of my stay in Treviso, I had some months earlier pre-arranged to rent an apartment, very conveniently located near the *Piazza dell'Umanesimo Latino* in the older, historic part of the city. The apartment was close to the University of Padua's *Scuolá di Giurisprudenza*, (law school), both located alongside Treviso's fast flowing and picturesque River Sile.

The idea here was to establish a base within the old part of the city. Here I planned to live and study, while at the same time also to document my past year of studies.

Organising the project

With some detailed planning and juggling of projects during the year before leaving for Italy, while forcing myself to save what I could from my limited income by not spending on a number of things that I really didn't need during the year, I found that I could just manage to finance my planned visit.

Apart from the airfare to get me to Italy in the first place, plus the extra cost of renting an apartment in which to base myself, I figured that living costs while in Italy could be kept to a manageable minimum.

Renting an apartment proved to be a lot less costly and much more convenient than staying in hotels. The cost involved with a month of tuition in Treviso also proved to be just about manageable.

Cooking regularly would also go a long way toward keeping down the cost of feeding myself, at the same time needing me to visit the local supermarket on a regular basis. With power and heating costs back home in Australia being kept to the absolute minimum, my home closed and the gas, power and water services unused or turned off during my absence, a longer stay could just become a possibility.

Local Australian costs for gas, electricity and water during my Italian stay would be close to zero, well below the high level of usage, particularly for the heating and power usually incurred during the usual three or four months of a Melbourne winter. Savings achieved there I calculated would just about allow the possibility of keeping my living expenses down to a manageable level.

The cost of feeding myself while resident proved lower than expected, even accounting for meals away from my rented apartment.

Organising a centrally located apartment was relatively easy, also surprisingly moderate in cost, having extensively surfed the Internet in search of an apartment to rent.

Renting accommodation in Italy

There are many rental agencies located in whichever city in Italy a visitor is planning to stay. The Airbnb site is one example of many other sources of accommodation availability.

Many private Italian owners offer apartments or houses owned personally or by the family for rental. Many others may even offer rooms within their own residence to rent.

Rental costs vary, usually according to the location and size of a particular property, the number of rooms and facilities provided in the form of furnishings, air-conditioning, cooking facilities, Wi-Fi access etc., and whether the accommodation is of modern construction, ancient or somewhere in-between. It will pay to do your research thoroughly, well in advance of any plans to visit.

Properties located in what is known as the *vecchia* (old) or *storico* (historical) part of a city location will usually cost more to rent than other properties on the outer periphery of a town or city.

If deciding upon an apartment or room on the outer edge of the city of your choice, you will also do well to make sure that public transport is close by, either in the form of train or bus.

The choice of a smaller city can be important here, as you will find that travel from the outer regions of a smaller city or provincial town is much easier to manage than trying to do the same in a larger principal Italian city like Rome, Milan, Naples or Florence.

On arrival in Treviso, I also arranged to rent a bicycle. The city offered a useful and economic bicycle rental service that should suit anyone staying within cycling distance of the language school they intend enrolling with. Similar services are also available in a number of other Italian cities.

It will pay to make any residential arrangements well before a planned visit, thus allowing for any interchange of phone messages or emails with the agency or private owner involved. You will invariably find that the more choice the location and apartment, the quicker it is liable to be taken up, so it pays to make your choice of accommodation, confirm and book well in advance of your stay.

For me it really came down to firming up on a location and environment with which I was familiar. The accommodation I had rented in Treviso also served to provide a broad range of travel possibilities, both in terms of rail and local bus services. The city also has easy access to air services, both internal and international. Also, there is the question of the range of interesting local features that can be visited while being based close to the selected language school.

A number of my Australian friends, and others I have met along the way, often tend to wax lyrical and enthusiastically about, Rome, Tuscany, the Amalfi coast, Cinque Terra or some other interesting region of Italy that they have either read about or actually visited, usually for just a few days or perhaps a full week or so during a past vacation.

The attractive title of a book written about a particular area, sometimes promoted by an enraptured celebrity, has on occasion left me less than impressed. This is particularly so when I have visited the same location the author had written about but found myself wondering why I could not share the author's obviously unbridled enthusiasm for the place.

Doesn't everyone have personal views on which region represents a more attractive location to visit?

Book titles like *Under the Tuscan Sun*, *A Castle in Tuscany* and a number of others written in a similar vein tend to extol the delights of that attractive and well-travelled region of Italy. While Tuscany is a province every visitor to Italy should plan to visit, the region cannot reasonably claim to possess all that is beautiful and interesting in Italy.

With this thought in mind therefore and without any intention of trying to influence anyone regarding my own preferences when deciding on places to visit in Italy, it was for me the Veneto province and the city of Treviso, at least for this visit.

Another way of looking at where to establish oneself, particularly if contemplating an longer visit to Italy for similar purposes as mine were for my visit in 2015, is to consider the size of the town or city in which you are planning to make your temporary residence.

The choice usually will be between setting up in a large city like Rome, Milan, Florence or Turin, as against one smaller, usually less costly but generally more convenient in terms of accommodation and living expenses. It would also be advisable to select a location more conducive to enabling you, as a temporary visitor, to make yourself more familiar with the location and local services, not forgetting the possibility of getting to know at least some of the local residents, or even your temporary neighbours, for the purpose of meeting new people and practicing your conversation skills.

This could prove to be more difficult staying in a large city like Rome, Milan or Florence, where many of the people you will usually meet while shopping or walking the streets, particularly during the summer vacation season, are likely to be non-Italian-speaking tourists.

In the end, it gets to be a matter of choice. Mine came out on the side of selecting the relatively small but interesting and easy to negotiate city of Treviso – at least the older part of the city, within its ancient walls and two encircling rivers and moat.

Let's face it, every region of Italy has its special claim to fame or infamy, always recognising that nearly every square kilometre of the country can lay some claim to having contributed at least something toward the developing history, not only of the country, but of Europe.

12. Seeing and doing around Treviso

Treviso – A brief history

Treviso was established and settled during the Bronze Age, first inhabited by people then known as Venetos and Celts. The city was conquered later by the Romans, who then turned it into a small city-state. Later, during the 14th century, Treviso came under the control of the Republic of Venice.

Treviso has been well known since the Middle Ages as the capital of a region called *Marca gioiosa et amorosa* (a province of joy and love) and seen as having been at the centre of a flourishing history of courtly love, poetry and literature. This feature of the city has continued to develop and flourish over many centuries, even to the present day.

The fertile soil and the abundance of water in what became the general area of the current province attracted a number of different peoples to the region, mainly earlier Gauls and Romans.

In 49 BC Treviso, formerly became known as Tarvisium, finally receiving a town charter as it flourished under Roman rule and law for the first time. In 396 AD, the city was elevated to the status of bishopric. Under the later Goths, Lombards and Carolingians, Treviso continued to flourish and became capital of the whole region.

Despite continuing prosperity, Treviso was unable to assert

its power against some of the more aggressive neighbouring cities. From 1237 on the city came under the rule of different Venetian neighbours. In 1339, it was conquered by the Doge's republic of Venice, becoming the first landward city to be established by the Venetians.

Later the Venetian princes and rich merchants built the *Via Terraglio*, a road connecting Venice with Treviso, along which still can be seen a few of the remaining beautiful villas and grand houses of then prosperous Venetians, many of whom also built vacation villas in Treviso itself.

Under the rule of Venice, Treviso experienced a renewed period of stability and prosperity – that was until 1797 when Austria assumed power over the province and ruled Treviso, with a couple of relatively short French interruptions, until 1866, following which it became a part of modern Italy.

The denomination *Marca Trevigiana* still commonly used, embraces territory encompassing Treviso and the surrounding hills and plain, a province of the same name dotted with medieval castles and ruined fortresses, the scenes of past feuds. There are many charming villages dotted across the province, all blessed with an enchanting natural setting, made up of rolling hills covered with vineyards, olive groves, cornfields and orchards.

Others may say with some conviction, "*so can you also describe many other places, the length and breadth of Italy*", and that of course may well be true.

From the perspective of this traveller, however, the Veneto province and the older parts of the city of Treviso, offered a little more and in a very subtle way, although I will readily admit that I have not visited everywhere there is to see in Italy.

Being so limited, therefore, I bow to others' opinions as to the places among their travels in Italy that they have found to be just as attractive to them.

Treviso today presents an ideal starting point, should a visitor aim for a getaway toward the hills and uniquely shaped Dolomite mountains to the north, location of the small townships of Valdobbiadene and Prosecco, producing areas of the worldwide celebrated homonymous Prosecco[7] wine. Beside that, the tourist meccas of Venice, Padua, Verona, Cortina d'Ampezzo, Vicenza, Lake Garda and Trieste, the latter city itself located in the neighbouring province of Friuli–Venezia Giulia just to the east, are all easily reachable either by train, car or bus.

Talking about wines of the region, and the wine now widely known as Prosecco in particular, is all about a dry sparkling white wine, grown, harvested and bottled among the scenic hills in the so-called *Marca Trevigiana* in the north-eastern part of the province.

Prosecco wine has always been a top seller throughout Italy.

---

[7] "Prosecco is an Italian white wine. Prosecco DOC can be *spumante* ("sparkling wine"), *frizzante* ("semi-sparkling wine"), or *tranquillo* ("still wine"), depending on the perlage. It is made from Glera grapes, formerly known also as Prosecco, but other grape varieties may be included. The following varieties are traditionally used with Glera up to a maximum of 15% of the total: Verdiso, Bianchetta Trevigiana, Perera, Glera lunga, Chardonnay, Pinot Bianco, Pinot Grigio and Pinot Nero. The name is derived from that of the Italian village of Prosecco near Trieste, where the grape may have originated. Prosecco DOC is produced from nine provinces spanning the Veneto and Friuli Venezia Giulia regions. Prosecco Superiore DOCG comes in two varieties: Prosecco Conegliano Valdobbiadene Superiore DOCG, which can only be made in the Treviso province of Veneto on the hills between the towns of Conegliano and Valdobbiadene (north of Treviso), and the smaller Asolo Prosecco Superiore DOCG, produced near the town of Asolo." (Source: Wikipedia)

Over recent times it has also become popular in many other countries across the world, regarded by many wine aficionados as being equal to or perhaps, according to some leading sommeliers, even more favoured than the famous French Champagne district wines of a similar style.

The hills that produce Prosecco wine are every bit as impressive as the Veneto's other great wine production region, the Valpolicella. Located in the western part of the province the Valpolicella produces its superb Amarone wines. The hills in both regions are unique, gentle and at times steep, thick with vineyards, rows upon rows clothing their sloping terrain.

The countryside around Treviso also offers great hospitality, with a number of *agriturismi* (local country style hotels serving fresh produce, mainly of their own production) and bed-and-breakfast properties that often happen to be beautifully restored country houses, many located in some of the more picturesque spots around the city.

Treviso being a small city, its historic centre is quite easily explored on foot. Whereas the province of Treviso, which includes a broad range of country and local townships around the old city, has a population of around 900,000, estimates of the population living within the city's ancient walls are less than 80,000 (ref: Wikipedia).

During the Second World War the Allies carried out regular bombing runs into Italy, with many into the Veneto attacking cities like Verona and Vicenza, in addition to Treviso

Treviso was hit very hard, being seriously damaged by many violent bombing raids. The most serious damage was suffered by the city on just one terrible day, 7 April 1944 during an aerial bombing campaign that caused the death of 2,000 local people. Even today, you can find references to the bombings of that period in wall posters and murals, permanently displayed across the city.

Piazza dei Signori

The piazza, central to the old part of the city is an always lively, central square, with nearby cafés bars, boutiques and a variety of other kinds of shops. The piazza forms a general meeting point for the people of Treviso, including visitors who will usually make for it in the evening, perhaps for a pizza at the world famous *Da Pino* pizza restaurant.

It is a classical Italian piazza, where you will normally see people strolling around or sitting outdoors at a bar table or under the piazza's portico sipping a coffee, a glass of Prosecco wine or spritz. Some just like to sit around, maybe pecking at the typical Venetian's finger food, the so-called *cicchetti* or any one of a variety of *tramezzini* (sandwiches), or just watching the parade of people passing by.

Some say that watching people passing by is one of most Italians' favourite pastimes. That is particularly so during the daytime where you will also see some of the more elderly male locals sitting in the piazza and chatting, as they ogle the passing throng of young, attractive women as they flit from boutique to boutique around the inner city.

The piazza is also the site of some interesting buildings, like the crenelated *Palazzo del Podestà*, and the *Torre del Comune*, a 48-metre high tower. The most significant building of *Piazza dei*

Signori is the *Palazzo dei Trecento*, whose name means "Palace of the Three Hundreds". The name originates from the fact that in the Middle Ages this palace would host the City Council, made up of 300 citizens, 50% nobles and 50% belonging to the lower classes of local citizens. It is a big medieval building with arcades and a portico hosting bar tables and occasionally, assemblies.

A unique fountain, medieval alleyways

Tucked away in a small courtyard to the rear of the *Palazzo dei Trecento*, sits a quite unusual, some might regard more in the way of a somewhat confronting, perhaps suggestive fountain, the *Fontana delle Tette*. I am not sure as to the sculptor, nor the significance of this perhaps confronting piece of art, but it always seems to attract a great deal of attention and interest from visiting tourists, as well as some of the locals.

Not far from the *duomo* there are many streets lined with porticoes, many having been built alongside a picturesque canal. Entering the back alleys it is important not miss the cobblestoned *via del Gallo* for a kind of imaginary return to what the city would have looked like during the Middle Ages. You won't find noble palaces there now, but houses that used to belong to lower class citizens during medieval times.

The Church of *San Nicolò*, one of the most significant monuments of the town, dates back to the late 1200s. Here a visitor may take advantage of a free visit to the cloister and most of all to the *Sala del Capitolo*, decorated with fine and precious 14th century frescoes representing forty of the most illustrious friars belonging to the Dominican order. Interesting also is the fact that one of the friars is depicted wearing what looks to be a pair of reading glasses: This may be the first representation of glasses in art history?

Pescheria, antique water mills

This area in the authentic older part of Treviso is dotted with *osterie* and typical food and wine stores. Upon a small island there you will also find the uniquely positioned *pescheria* (fish market) and nearby, some of the city's old water wheels.

Surrounding the *citta vecchia* (old city) within the *muro* (city wall), itself skirted on the outside by what used to be the city moat, you can virtually walk around most of the inner city along what was the top of the old city wall, now converted into a tree-lined boulevard.

Upon this wall, particularly during the summer months (July/August) you can attend Treviso's *Ferragosto* (Assumption day holiday) celebrated each year on 15th August, and Treviso's famous *Suoni di Marca*. This is a two-week-long festival in July/August that every evening features groups of different bands, orchestras and singers in a continuous *festa* (celebration) of music, with food *bancarelle* (stalls) and a whole host of other stalls selling anything from drinks, food, spices and pottery.

In short, it is correct, even today, to describe Treviso as a city which both historically and in the present, possesses the spirit that continues to make it a *Marca Gioiosa et Amorosa*.

I have loved just being there, living, studying and writing – in addition to taking a regular *gita in bicicletta* (bicycle ride) along the River Sile, followed by *pranzo* (lunch) in the picturesque township of Casier sul Sile, just a few kilometres downstream

After all that ... did my Italian improve?

By the time late August 2015 came around it was time to bid farewell to Treviso, new-found friends and one or two much valued and longer known. I must say that the value of actually taking time out to experience living like an Italian local and using the Italian language in Italy really did work for me.

It was hard work at first, but the full three months spent living Italian-style, while forcing me to resist using or trying not to think in English, served to enable me to begin breaking through the wall that earlier had resisted progress toward a higher level of language acquisition.

Not only did I gain a great deal more in Italian vocabulary, I also found myself, in spite of a few nervous days at the start, actually beginning to feel more confident when called upon to conduct a conversation or on being asked a question. It even got to the point where I was getting to be regarded as a regular at one or two of the local bars, and finding myself greeted as such when I entered to order my usual *caffé latte e una brioche*. That alone was surely a sign that I was becoming accepted, even with my 'funny' non-Italian accent and often suspect grammar!

As the weeks passed, I felt I was getting closer to the point of becoming capable of hearing and answering friends and even strangers with whom I found myself speaking along the way. The longer time went by, so did my Italian improve to the point, either during a conversation or finding myself in a situation requiring an exchange of information, that I was able to answer, often without feeling the need to stop and think.

I have still yet to be able to conduct a great deal more than an everyday kind of conversation in Italian. Perhaps more importantly, though, I was finding myself at long last being able to literally 'let go of the bar' as described earlier, and allowing myself to float free from the fear of not being able to find the correct words or phrases. I began to feel myself entering into a a more relaxed state, that as time passed gradually enabled me to think more immediately in Italian. This was a major breakthrough that allowed me greater freedom, instead of always stumbling while having to slowly translate from English what it was I wanted to communicate.

Realising that I had the capacity to do so when it happened was satisfying and worth all the hours spent in study and practice, achieved while working exclusively on my own for the past year!

I also found that due to the efforts put in during the year before my arrival in Italy and the more I forced myself to speak, ask questions and join in conversations with friends and others along the way, the better I found myself able to do so. At last, I was beginning to feel as though I was on the cusp of speaking with a great deal more freedom – at the same time with less fear of making too many mistakes.

It wasn't easy at first, but as they say in Italy, *poco a poco* (little by little) I began to find myself using words and phrases in discussion which, while often not always being what one could consider fluent, did allow me to listen to and answer strangers met in the street, restaurant or bar, as and when conversation or enquiry became necessary. This sometimes required me to advise that I was in the process of learning their language together with the request "please can you speak a little slower".

The improvement from a year before was a revelation, and one that had me even extending myself to attempting to take part in explanations and dialogues, sometimes with success and other times not. Regardless, it didn't seem to matter even if I did make mistakes. That factor alone really excited me to the extent that it served to fire up my desire to improve still further.

Unfortunately time ran out and I had to leave Italy – all too soon finding myself once again back in Australia, now with the aim of trying to hold onto the range of Italian vocabulary I had gained. This while continuing to work toward absorbing more knowledge about Italy and Italian, so that by my next visit I should be able to build further on my improving ability to hold a conversation.

The visit also proved successful in another way when it came to reviewing what I had learned, and assessing how successful my yearlong programme of self-tuition had been in preparing me for my 2015 visit.

The programme that had developed as a result of earlier research, once initiated and followed through, had proved to be effective. This was mainly because I refused to allow myself at any time during the year to drop back from regular study, constant practice and carefully planned coordination – across each element of my programme.

The Pimsleur audio aid in particular deserves a mention here, particularly as it was and continues to be the core aid I will keep on using. While other elements of the programme, such as reading texts, listening to radio, counting and calculating in Italian and the regular practice of 'talking to myself' have been beneficial, it was the use of an interactive audio programme like Pimsleur that naturally assumed the central role around which other elements of the programme became woven.

In conclusion

To return to the original question posed by this book "Why should I learn to speak Italian?" My inclination is to counter it with a firm "Why not?"

It could be argued that while some of the reasons offered in support of learning Italian, similar to those put by Flinders University, could be put aside without attracting too many complaints, it would be difficult to ignore the various other university study groups and perhaps other medical research teams' arguments in support of the value to be gained with learning to become bilingual. Apart from any other consideration, for me studying Italian has opened yet another door to a useful and rewarding skill – one of being able to speak with at least some success in a language other than my native English.

The ability to communicate in more than one language offers any individual who might just be contemplating such a journey, a unique window through which to view the wonderful world in which we live, but now from a different standpoint.

The capacity to speak in a second language also offers the possibility of learning a great deal more about a nation and people other than our own. While doing so, acquisition of a second language, along with the possibility of actually getting to use it in the country of one's choice, will also provide a unique opportunity to experience life and living as practiced by people having a different culture to our own – who follow a different way of thinking and way of life.

The question posed in this book, though, was specific: "Why Italy, and why learn Italian?"

I am hoping that by the time you have reached this page, the answer to that question will have already emerged, even if you remain to be convinced. You may also now be able to realise some of the value to be gained when deciding to commit to what could prove to be a difficult and frustrating journey.

When it comes to any discussion on or around the question of "why Italy" when measured against that of any other country, then I guess it just becomes one of an individual's preference.

Think on it! Of all the places on the face of the earth, which one appeals to you the most? If the answer to that turns out to be China or perhaps Japan, France, Vietnam, Sweden, Spain, Russia, Iceland or some other non-English-speaking culture, then my suggestion is to go for it. Make the decision to learn the language and while doing so, aim also to learn more about the country's history, its unique culture, the way the people think and live their lives, then make the decision to become proficient with its language. You will not regret it.

The decision to take out at least some form of insurance against the possibility of an early descent into the kind of mental problems besetting an increasing number of older citizens is surely worth some consideration, if only to ease our minds.

If what an increasing number of medical researchers are saying is to be believed, taking up the study of a second language could well prove to be the difference between the earlier or much later risk of receiving a premature visit from a group of pernicious mental demons – in this case, the fear of becoming trapped prematurely in the prison of failing mental health.

I chose Italy for my journey. My choice had nothing to do with the possibilities raised by Flinders University, my future mental health or any other of the reasons referred to earlier.

I chose Italy and decided on Italian from among the many different countries I had visited over a long and varied business career. I chose it because of what the country represented in a historical and philosophical sense. But I chose it mainly because every day I am able to spend there serves to uncover the same kind of emotions I used to feel as a young boy – a period during which my earlier years and rapidly expanding experiences of life began to unveil the thrill of living in an amazingly diverse, fascinating world. Italy presents to me as a country and people that I hope to continue visiting while continuing to learn more of its language and culture.

Italy is a unique place, the inheritor of a long, unique and fascinating story – a country possessing something special, a language that continues to challenge me: *la lingua più bella del mondo.*

13. References and information

You will find any number of providers of courses and all kinds of aids to learning Italian on both the Internet and among language bookshops throughout the world. Some will offer courses and materials using either, or a combination of texts and audio, to teach the language.

Most courses, when you really get down to the nitty-gritty of what they are offering, are often similar in nature, with variations between them mainly in the form that their material is presented.

When it comes to tutoring services, individual language tutors – some working from their home base in Italy, may offer to work with foreign students via the Internet, usually via Skype, for a fee. Others based in a student's home country are usually in a position to offer a variety of courses or services on a more personal, in-situ basis.

There are a number of teachers and schools specialising in Italian to be found in most major cities across Australia and other English-speaking countries, each offering their particular brand of language education. Details and addresses of these are best accessed via your local telephone services directory, or via the Internet. When it comes to choice, it will usually be a case of trying to select the kind of service and provider you feel comfortable with. Of course, if choosing a provider but having little in the way of previous information on that provider, it will be a case of trial-and-error. If possible, preferably try out a few options before getting yourself too heavily involved with any one language service provider.

I am limiting the details of courses and any comments on other learning aids noted in this section to those I have personally tried at some time or another. Where appropriate, I have already noted those services and aids that I found to be of more assistance in improving my capacity to learn, retain and later use most of the material thus learned in conversation.

There will of course be many other individuals or organisations, both locally based and in Italy, who offer courses similar to those I have included. Some of these services may well have been found to be of assistance to other students.

The point here is that you should try to do your own research, both locally and on the Internet. Try, wherever possible, to obtain an independent review of any services before making a commitment – preferably before paying for their use.

The following information is provided for your consideration as a starter in your quest to learn or improve your already commenced studies in Italian. Also provided is an email address through which I may be contacted, should you wish to offer an opinion on the content included in this book.

I wish here to acknowledge a number of Internet sites and other sources of public information used during research for this book, the following but two among them:

Standard Italian (not) Spoken Here

http://italian.about.com/od/linguistics/a/aa082008a.htm

This is a useful site, readily available on the Internet and provided by Michael San Filippo. The site was used, in part and among other sources, as a reference to the history of Standard Italian.

News in Slow Italian (NewsInSlowItalian.com)

This is an Internet-based source of Italian news, creatively arranged to provide a reasonably up to date record of Italian news. It is presented in an interactive format. The site provides a non-Italian reader with a novel way by which to access a translation of Italian news reports into English, in addition to providing a reading in Italian of the information provided.

This and other similar Internet sites offer various ways to extend a student's level of understanding of Italian, both written and verbal.

Articles on the benefits of learning a second language

An internet search will uncover a range of articles dealing with different aspects of this subject. There is not much in the way of doubt that undertaking the study of a second language can have a number of benefits, which, according to some experts in the field, are worthy of close study and understanding.

The following are summaries of just three different views on the subject. Each one of the articles referenced is worth reading in full at the address provided.

"The benefits of learning a second language", Professor Jennifer Smith

www.omniglot.com/language/articles/benefitsoflearningalanguage.htm

Jennifer Smith is a professor of sociolinguistics at the University of Glasgow, and provides a comprehensive review of the sociological benefits that that are to be discovered by someone considering the acquisition of a second language. In this extensive article, she gives a number of cogent reasons for commencing study of a second language.

Smith points out that whatever a person's age, being bilingual has its advantages, especially in today's global society.

Areas where she believes learning another language is of particular benefit include the following:

- **Better job prospects.** In today's business-dominated society, and with many companies planning to expand into overseas markets, often a bilingual person may prove more successful.

- **Brain health.** The acquisition of a second language has been shown to delay the onset of many brain-related diseases, Alzheimer's and dementia among them.

- **Travel and leisure.** Being able to speak a language other than one's own can offer travellers or business people the advantage of not being troubled with the need for translations, particularly where the visitor has gained some proficiency in the local language.

- **Improved first language.** The study and learning of a second language can also focus attention on one's own native language and the structure of its grammar.

- **Improved understanding of the world.** Smith believes that learning a new language provides for a greater understanding of the world we live in. She points to such things as gaining access to new films, music and literature, together with a greater appreciation of the history and culture of a new country, and a better understanding of the way the world works, particularly in areas like politics and security.

- **Experience new cultures.** The professor maintains that the world is "a cauldron of rich and interesting cultures". She gives a number of examples of the new experiences available to someone who has opened themselves to a culture other than their native one.

- **Achievement.** Smith points out that "learning a new language is an achievement anyone can be proud of". She also makes the important point that "learning a new language will open up a new world in ways a monolingual person would never have the chance of experiencing".

"Being bilingual 'protects brain'," BBC News

http://news.bbc.co.uk/2/hi/health/3794479.stm

On 15 June 2004, the BBC reported on a study carried out on over 100 people between the ages of 30 and 38 by York University in Canada. This study found that those fluent in two languages rather than one were mentally sharper.

The journal *Psychology and Aging* reported that the university researchers had found that being bilingual might protect against mental decline in old age. Previous studies had also shown that keeping the brain active could protect against senile dementia. It was also commented that people who play musical instruments, dance or read regularly could be less likely to develop the condition. Other activities requiring some level of concentration, like playing board games or crosswords, were also thought to assist.

When it comes to language skills, the York University study also appears to back up the theory that the acquisition of a second language can have a protective effect. To assess the cognitive skills of those who were involved with the study, Dr Ellen Bialystok and a number of her colleagues used a variety of widely recognised tests. Half the volunteers came from Canada and could speak only English, while the other half were from India, and fluent in both Tamil and English. All the volunteers were tested on their vocabulary skills, non-verbal reasoning ability and reaction times. The volunteers had similar backgrounds, all being middle class and educated to degree level.

The researchers found that those who were fluent in both English and Tamil responded faster than those who were fluent in just English. This applied across all age groups.

It is also interesting that the researchers found the bilingual subjects were less likely to suffer mental decline associated with old age, stating that, "The bilingual volunteers were more efficient at all ages tested and showed a slower rate of decline for some processes with ageing", adding that "it appears that bilingualism helps to offset age-related losses."

The BBC went on to report that Professor Clive Ballard, director of research for the UK's Alzheimer's Society, had welcomed the research, saying that "these findings [indicate] that early development of a second language may improve a specific aspect of cognitive function in later life". The professor went on to say, "It is a possibility that the acquisition of a second language in early childhood may also influence the process of the development of neuronal circuits." But he added, on a cautious note, that the results of that particular research needed to be interpreted cautiously, "as the research was comparing groups of individuals of different nationalities, educated in different systems, [and] it is also well recognised that education in general can bestow benefits on cognitive function (cognition) in later life."

This BBC report is recommended reading to anyone that might be thinking about taking up the study of a second language. Its findings were accepted and cautiously endorsed by the UK's Alzheimer's Society, and there does appear to be sufficient evidence in it to support taking up the study of a second language.

I, at least, am one 'struggling student' who over the past year or so has found myself taxing my brain and its capacity to in the hope of absorbing and actually speaking a completely different language to the only one I had spoken for in excess of a half century!

I am not sure if this qualifies me for a delay in whatever the gods have in store for me as a 'senior citizen', but if the Canadian university's findings prove to be correct, I may well have bought myself perhaps a few more months or even years before the inevitable downturn in cognitive function finally gets the better of me. As they say in Italy – *Magari!* (maybe!).

"How long does it take to learn a new language?", Dr Sarah Eaton

https://drsaraheaton.wordpress.com/…/how-long-does-it-take-to-learn-a-new-language

In this article, Sarah Eaton goes into a great deal of detail in discussing the amount of time required to learn a second language. She starts by saying that most language teachers will tell you that "what you put in is what you will get out of language studies". She also points out that companies that sell language-learning products or software may claim that their products will guarantee fluency in a certain period of time, and that that time frame just happens to correspond to the length of their particular programme.

She points out here that language experts tend to be sceptical about claims that a certain method can guarantee fluency in a short period of time. She then gives a number of reasons why most of those involved with the study of language learning hold this view:

- **The age of the learner.** Eaton cites a study that shows, "If second-language acquisition begins at age 5, it follows a different pattern than when second-language acquisition begins at age 25 or at age 15."

- **Immersion.** This relates to whether "a minority or a majority language". If you are living in an English-speaking country and learning Italian, you are learning a minority language. This makes the learning process different.

- **Language learning in school.** The article notes "students that take foreign-language classes in school are unable to to receive sufficient exposure to the language to gain deep fluency".

- **Language learning in terms of hours.** Under this heading, Dr Eaton provides a number of different scenarios, compared to what she describes as the "10,000-hour rule". In these, she discusses and calculates in detail how different levels of study per week match up to the above rule, which was based on a research study originally published in the *Harvard Business Review*,[8] which puts forward the idea that it takes 10,000 hours of practice to become expert at a skill. The book *Outliers* by Malcolm Gladwell, helped popularise this notion.

The different language-learning scenarios described by Dr Eaton in her article range across a number of headings, including "adult education classes", "foreign-language studies at school", "dedicated self-study", and "total immersion". On this last scenario, she says,

> Some argue that immersion is the "best" way to learn a language. Others argue that there is no one "best" way. It

---
[8]Ericsson, K. A., Prietula, M. J., & Cokely, E. T. "The Making of an Expert," *Harvard Business Review* (July–August 2007).

may not be about the methods used, but simply about the amount of hours spent learning. Learning can be done in formal, non-formal or informal contexts. Language learning doesn't always take place in the classroom. Trained teachers can offer strategies and guidance that the self-directed learner may not have.

Italian courses

Centre of Italian Studies (CIS)
247–249 Cardigan Street, Carlton, Victoria 3053.
Telephone: (03) 9347 9144
Internet: CIS@italianstudies.com.au

On its website, the CIS states that since its foundation in 1979, it has been committed to providing students of all ages with quality Italian language education. There will be other, similar organisations offering courses in Italian in or around your home location. The CIS also claims that it will have students speaking Italian from day one—a claim discussed and discounted earlier in this book. It also claims expertise in the field of language teaching, having developed a number of courses such as "Avanti" and "Sempre Avanti", which they claim are being widely used throughout Australia and around the world.

Located in the Italian-dominated suburb of Carlton, just north of the Melbourne CBD, the CIS is recognised as one of Australia's leading schools of Italian studies, but its location limits accessibility to those students living within reasonable proximity of its address. As also discussed earlier, I found that the CIS and other similar schools are limited in their capacity to provide all the means by which a serious student of Italian may achieve a workable degree of real fluency in the language. Nevertheless, CIS does offer excellent facilities to its students, with native Italian speakers providing all its tutorial services.

The CIS notes that the features it offers include:

- Lively and entertaining courses
- A programme based on sound educational principles
- A wide range of class times and levels designed to allow maximum flexibility
- A committed team of expert teachers, all with native fluency
- A lounge area where students may relax
- A bookshop stocking a range of Italian educational publications
- Competitive rates and value for money
- Small class sizes

I found the CIS programme very helpful, particularly during the earlier stages of basic grammar and language acquisition. For me, though, the school's lack of capacity to provide much beyond the intermediate level, particularly when it came to absorbing, thinking and speaking Italian, reduced its value considerably. I should add that the same applied to other schools offering classroom-based Italian tuition.

Co.As.It
Sydney based Italian language and community-based services
Internet: coasit.org.au
Phone: (02) 9564 0744

Note: Co.As.It is a similar kind of organisation to CIS in Melbourne, also offering language services to students based in and around Sydney.

Universita per Stranieri, Perugia, Italy (UpS)
Address: Piazza Fortebraccio 4, Perugia 06123, Italy.
Telephone: +39 075 57461
Internet: www.unistrapg.it/en

Established in 1921, Universita per Stranieri claims to be the oldest university oriented to Italian studies for foreign students. Its so styled 'Erasmus' summer courses generally run around 10–28 August each year, with a 3-week intensive course 31 August–18 September.

The university, like most other Italy-based courses, usually can also offer to arrange residential accommodation during the student's stay. By all means, try spending some time at this university, but be aware that the groups that you attend may well be larger and therefore less able to provide a more interactive form of tuition than a smaller school or service would usually be capable of.

E.STI.VE Eurostudi Treviso
"Scuola di lingua e cultura Italian"
Address: Vicolo Barberia 9, Treviso 13100, Italy
Telephone: (+39) 3425 590839
Internet: eurostudi@italiaservice.com

This school provided what I found to be a well-balanced course in Italian, which included tuition in both grammar and conversational Italian, all of which was presented in a useful and entertaining manner. While concentrating initially on the various grammar forms necessary when constructing the required level of Italian, the course also strove to develop the students' confidence when using what they had been taught as part of everyday living in an Italian environment.

The course is highly recommended. Intending students can also arrange accommodation through the school to whichever level suits their needs and pocket, in and around the inner city area of Treviso. This ranges from a private apartment, through to other less individual accommodation and hotel rooms.

"Mani in Pasta" one-on-one learning

The following is background to the system of learning developed by its now Melbourne-based founder, Italian-educated language mentor Federica Mattiuzzo.

Phone: 0412 108 788
Email: federica.mattiuzzo@gmail.com

Learning any new language can at the best of times, become difficult and boring. This I believe is primarily so because of the perceived need to undertake hours of often tedious study in order to come to grips with basic Italian grammar; words and verbs – and their various conjugations – all this prior to becoming capable of conducting even a basic level of conversation. The process tends to become a long one, unless the student has the additional assistance of family at home. Even then the learning process tends to be uninteresting and bereft of any form of enjoyable connection.

I have for some time studied and practiced the teaching of Italian to foreign students, both adults and children. The way in which my course developed was from the realisation that trying to learn a second language in a static fashion, sitting in a chair for example as a part of a class or group for one or perhaps two hours at a time, falls far short of integrating the teaching with one or other "fun" or other form of relaxing involvement designed to suit a particular students' preferences. In other words learning – while at the same time having some fun or other activity of interest to the student. The fun aspect of my course is important, particularly when working with children.

Such activity is the means used to both positively engage and enhance a student's learning process. The system I have developed really works, and I have found that my students quickly become more familiar with the various forms of grammar and Italian idiom as a result. The learning of grammar and other important aspects of the language are closely integrated into the learning process, as each stage is introduced and eventually reached by the student.

Pimsleur Italian

This course produced and marketed by Simon & Schuster Audio, provided as a collection of audio programmes accompanied by reference texts, can also be accessed by direct download onto either of an iPhone, iPad or other similar cellular device or desktop computer. The courses provided, range from level 1 (Basic) to level 5 (Advanced), are well designed and considered to provide excellent support for anyone wishing to gain more in the way of practical conversation assistance. The way in which the various levels are structured proved superior to other similar kinds of audio services, one or two of which I have also referred to earlier. Highly recommended.

Italian textbooks

There are a whole host of different kinds of textbooks, some purely text while others also include CDs intended to be used in conjunction with the supplied written material.

Contemporary children's books are also a good way to build up a student's knowledge of Standard Italian, with this kind of book written in a relatively simple form, easily read by anyone with more than just a basic level of Italian at their disposal.

A comprehensive Italian/English dictionary is a must here, as is a comprehensive book of Italian verbs having an English explanation. If attending one or other organisation-based training courses, they will no doubt recommend their preferred textbook, which they require to be used with their teaching methods and programme. These vary considerably, so it is best to discuss this with the course manager concerned before purchasing what they think may be useful as a text guide for their course.

Some books on Italian grammar

There are a number of books dealing with Italian grammar regularly being offered on the market. While I have over the years tried quite a few of them, I found one textbook in particular – *A Progressive Italian Grammar* – referred to earlier, to be of more assistance to me than any other. I am not certain if, while the book has been revised and reprinted over a number of years, it is still in print at the time of writing.

I have seen it advertised for sale on a number of websites. I have also come across second-hand copies in a few bookshops around Melbourne so it shouldn't be difficult to obtain a copy, should you wish to own one. It is a highly recommended textbook, which I still use as a reference on a regular basis.

Italianissimo

This particular series of books, published by Thomas Nelson and Sons Ltd. in the UK, has also been in print for a number of years, having been first published in 1992. Written fully in Italian, it seeks to cover all levels of its subject, using both text and photographs to represent the various areas of everyday living in Italy that each section and level of the textbook is seeking to illustrate.

This and similar publications, some printed later than *Italianissimo*, would be more useful for more advanced students as an additional reference, to their study of the language. The Italian used is relatively simple, but for a beginner would be a little difficult to follow.

CIAO

This particular series of books was first published by BBC Books in 1994, and followed a series of popular television programmes of the same name. The series was filmed and recorded for the BBC Continuing Education television and radio series "Italianissimo 2", the programme being first broadcast from January 1994.

Written in both English and Italian, the course follows on a similar theme to that of *Italianissimo*. It also seeks to cover subjects of study in Italian ranging from the very basic up to reasonably advanced levels.

Since publication of the above two series of textbooks, there are others which are currently available on the language learning market, some including CDs, produced in a format also recommended by the publishers, to be used as a supplement to the written text to better acclimatise the student to the use of Italian in an audio sense.

Scuola d'Italiano textbooks

I have found the range of books being published by this Italian organisation, which became available much later than both *Italianissimo* and *CIAO*, to be very useful, particularly for more advanced students. Two texts in particular are recommended.

Dizionario Italiano per Stranieri
(480 pages of indispensable words)

This particular dictionary, presented totally in Italian, serves to describe the meaning of a broad range of regularly used Italian words, in Italian. The English explanation of the words described in this dictionary will enable a reasonably advanced Italian student to understand the meaning and usage of a particular word or phrase. This kind of dictionary, although written totally in Italian, is a good reference book to have on hand. This particular publication will be of more benefit to a more advanced student of Italian.

Parlo Italiano – Manuali practici per stranieri

This manual, also presented totally in Italian, uses illustrations and text to describe a wide range of different situations and areas of everyday Italian life. It comes with a CD that can be used to reference the various texts. Once again, this will be very useful to reasonably advanced Italian students. This manual also includes a series of simple tests, following on from the various sections covered by the text and illustrations.

This publisher also puts out an extensive variety of more basic textbooks along the same lines as the above.

Two useful books written in English

La bella figura by Beppe Severgnini

This book takes the reader on a hilarious tour of modern Italy that takes you behind the seductive face the country puts on for visitors, in the author's terms – *la bella figura* – and uncovers the far more complex true self of the Italians. Being Italian himself, the author is writing from experience so, alongside his writing around some of the historic cities and descriptions of Italian countryside, there'll be stops at the places where the Italians reveal themselves in all their authentic, maddening glory:

the airport, the motorway and the bedroom.

Published by Hodder & Stoughton in 2008
ISBN 978 0 340 93603 0

Italian Ways by Tim Parks

Through memorable encounters with ordinary Italians – conductors and ticket collectors, priests and prostitutes, scholars and lovers, gypsies and immigrants – Tim Parks captures what makes Italian life distinctive. He explores how trains helped build Italy and how the railways reflect Italian's sense of themselves from Garibaldi to Mussolini to Berlusconi and beyond.

Tim, as you will gather, is not a native Italian but an English professor who has lived for a long period in Italy. He describes his experiences there in a broad ranging and interesting way.

Published by Vintage Books in 2014
ISBN 9780099584254

There are of course any number of other similar books, each providing a useful commentary on things Italian.

* * *

The following are details of a number of other different sources of assistance in Italian studies that you may also wish to contact or research further.

Italian learning systems online

Following are a selection of a few of the different kinds of courses and learning systems, currently on offer on the Internet.

Babbel (babbel.com)

This is one of a few systems that offers the opportunity it claims as being … "The fun and easy way to learn Italian". My only comment here is to go there and have a look at this programme – but be prepared to need much more than this site appears to offer

Rosetta Stone (rosettastone.com)

This site makes the offer at the time of writing: *"Now just $US229. Learn Italian with the new and improved Rosetta Stone"*. The site also offers the opportunity of a *"Trial Demo"* and goes on to add:

> With the Rosetta Stone method, you'll speak Italian from the very first lesson". This, like the earlier claim made by CIS, is a questionable claim in my view, unless of course a student is just interested in gaining a few simple to learn and hold Italian words and phrases.

There is a whole world of difference between being able to mouth a few words and phrases as against actually being able at the very least to carry on a simple conversation in Italian. The course as claimed may be able to provide a user with the former, but from my experience, it will take much more to achieve the latter.

Note: It should be stated here that users of the Rosetta Stone programme may well have found it satisfactory to them. The comments being offered here and elsewhere in this publication, relate only to the writer's experience – they should be read as such.

Italian learning system reviews

There is also at least one site that offers to provide reviews of the various Italian language learning systems on offer via the Internet. This site calls itself *Top 10 Reviews*.

Among the top sites recommended by this site, at the time of writing, are:

- Tell Me More Italian (a site understood to have been acquired by Rosetta Stone)
- Italian Complete Edition
- Pimsleur Italian Unlimited
- Rosetta Stone
- Berlitz

Like most other sites offering their services, it will pay to treat all such sites and offers with caution and do your homework before making a commitment to any one of them. All, in some way will provide you with assistance along the road. However, bear in mind that regardless of which kind of learning programme you choose to access and use, there will be no substitute for actually practicing what you have learned – on a daily basis, and with at least some time later spent in an Italian environment.

Other Internet sites detailing Italian schools and services in Italy

Studyabroad.com

This site provides details of various study courses and programmes offered in Italy, located in both smaller towns/cities and major cities. It also details the different types of programme categories, among them:

- Academic year
- Full degree
- Gap year etc.

www.babilonia.it/italianlanguage

This site offers to teach Italian in Italy. Its courses also include the possibility of linking tuition in Italian to other subjects, i.e.: "Italian + Cooking, Pottery, Diving, Hiking, Biking, Golf, Club 50… plus others."

www.ldminstitute.com ("Lorenzo de' Medici")

LdM promotes itself as being a private institution of higher education, located in Florence, with smaller campuses in other parts of Tuscany, Rome and Venice. The institute offers courses in both Language and Italian culture.

www.dantealigheri.com

Yes, of course there had to be at least one course in Italian using that famous name in Italian literature as its title. This organisation is primarily based in Siena and offers the comment: *"Where to study Italian language and culture in Italy. Siena the perfect city for Italian immersion programs and internships in Italy"* ... Need I add more?

www.scuolaleonardo.com

This school offers the opportunity to "learn Italian in Italy" and offers courses in Florence, Rome, Milan, Viareggio.

ItalianPod101.com

"Learn Italian the fastest and most fun way" is the way this service offers itself. Its Internet page goes on to say "It takes seconds to sign up and you will be speaking Italian in seconds more".

Need I comment further?

A couple of hours spent on the Internet will provide a number of other Italian learning programmes and aids. With the apparent popularity of Italian, the Internet will provide access to the full range of Italian related courses and learning products, available both in Italy and other countries... *Buona Fortuna* with your search...

The Veneto and the province of Treviso

The city featured earlier in this book, Treviso, and the surrounding territory bearing its name as the Province of Treviso, has much to offer the traveller. Apart from its long history, modern-day Treviso has been known throughout the ages as *Marca gioiosa et amorosa* (a province of joy and love). The city is ideally placed by its proximity to Venice, just a twenty-minute local train ride to the south, the picturesque Lake Garda to the east and the magnificent Dolomite ranges and the slopes of Valdobbiadene, Prosecco wine country, to the north.

The province of Treviso

Contained within the Veneto is the province of Treviso. The province forms an important part of the Veneto, encompassing much of the plain to the north of Venice, reaching just beyond Vittorio Veneto to the north and the stunning hill town of Asolo to the west.

The province is surrounded by the Prealps, the Dolomites, Venice, the beach-resort towns of Jesolo and Caorle and much more in every other direction. Treviso is serviced by two local airports: Canova Airport, just a few kilometres from the centre of Treviso, and Marco Polo Airport to the south, just to the east of Venice. It is also easily connected by rail to most of the major destinations throughout Italy and beyond into other parts of Europe, Croatia and the Dalmatian coast.

The Veneto

The province of Treviso is hospitable and genuine, as is the warmth of its people. Strangers are welcomed and you will no doubt be invited to partake in the local cuisine and the excellent DOC and DOCG wines, typical products of the province with IGP and DOP denomination.[9] The province, also known as the Marca Trevigiana, is difficult to describe in a few words. Every town, with its ancient walls, medieval villages and historical palaces, tells its own history. The province is characterised by the presence of many ancient villas and magnificent residences of the seventeenth century, which belonged to the rich Venetian noble families, built along the Sile River and Via Terraglio, two ancient trade routes. Towns to the south of Treviso, like Mogliano and Preganziol, still retain some of the old structures related to agriculture, which have stood since ancient times.

The province of Treviso

There is so much more to tell about the province and city of Treviso, of which I have given a description earlier in the book. There is also much more to tell about other parts of the Veneto: its lakes, mountains and so many other natural attractions that it would take another book just to describe them in sufficient detail. Instead, please consider exploring the excellent internet guide to the region provided by the provincial tourism authority at www.marcadoc.com/tourist-information-treviso.

---

[9] These are Italian and European Union quality- and provenance-assurance schemes. DOC(G): *Denominazione di origine controllata (e Garantita)* (controlled [and guaranteed] designation of origin). DOP: *Denominazione di origine protetta* (protected denomination of origin). IGP: *indication géographique protégée* (protected geographical indication).